Persecution

2000:

PREPARING
THE
UNDERGROUND
CHURCH

Persecution 2000: Preparing the Underground Church

© Copyright 1999 by Michael Bunker and Steve Donaldson

Printed by Gilliland Printing, 1999

Cover Design by Imagine Creative Services

For speaking engagements for Michael Bunker or Steven Donaldson:

Phone: (806) 234-2086
Email: info@bunkersurvival.com

For additional books, videos or audios, contact:

The Prophecy Club®
P. O. Box 750234
Topeka, KS 66675

Phone: (785) 478-1112
Fax: (785) 478-1115
Internet: www.prophecyclub.com

Persecution 2000:

Preparing the Underground Church

by
Michael B. Bunker and
Steven Donaldson

Acknowledgments

Steve Donaldson:

This writing has been both a labor of love and sadness. Love because it is His love that has given birth to it, and sadness because it is necessary to write it. It is a commentary on the state of affairs in which we find ourselves as Christians, in an anti-Christian society.

The information written here is a compilation of excerpts from lectures and lessons I've presented over time to various groups, both Christian and non-Christian. During the past 12 years I have been increasingly burdened by the state of the Church in America, and the Christian family in particular. I have seen it coming for a long time, as humanist ideas have been spoon fed to the public and swallowed by the Christian community, we have become dependent upon a malevolent government, and weak church leadership. Compromise has become the order of the day and we have compromised ourselves all the way to our present condition.

It is time for Christians to stop the compromise and stand firmly obedient to the Lord of the universe, Jesus Christ. During these last days we must have the ability to obey our Lord without hesitation, and without regard for consequence, if we are to fulfill our purpose.

This writing will address our history, our present state of affairs, and will give the believer God's prescription to cure the illness that has infected His Bride. As we look at the institutional church, the government and the Christian family, you will see both the plan of the enemy, and the purpose of the Lord unveiled. You will see there is a divine purpose for you here and now.

It is my prayer you will also find communion with our Lord, and learn to obey without hesitation and without regard for consequence.

I would like to thank my Lord and Savior Jesus Christ for His mercy and grace during this writing. I would also like to thank my wife Donna for her patience and support during the many hours spent away from my regular duties around our home. She has been a real trooper and this could not have been accomplished without her. I would also like to thank a few special people in my life who will remain unnamed, but are aware of who they are. One in particular knows exactly what it has taken to put this material together on very short notice, has been with me step by step through this labor of love, and has become a 'wonder' to me. Lastly, I want to thank Michael Bunker for putting this project together, for working out all the details, and for seeing it through to completion.

May the Lord Bless and keep us for His purpose, His Bride, and as a Light to the world during the perilous days ahead.

Michael Bunker:

It would be easy to go overboard in offering my thanks to those who deserve it. First of all I thank Jesus Christ my Lord and Saviour, for pulling me out of the sewer of my hideous old life and giving me a new life: FOR FREE!

This book has been a joy and a learning experience. I thank those brave and courageous people whose works are quoted in this book for their love, commitment and obedience. I learned more about the world and my place in it by reading the works of more accomplished and qualified authors. I also saw the hideous side of Christian persecution through their honest and brutal portrayals of the truth of our current world.

I thank GOD for giving me my beautiful and gracious wife Danielle. Without her I would have fallen apart long ago. Thanks also to my parents who have exhibited patience above and beyond the call of duty towards their wayward if not prodigal son.

I thank the folks at Awarehouse in Lubbock, Texas for giving Steve and I a forum through which to express these ideas. I thank Richard, Tom, Cloyce, Wayson, Stan, Sonny, JD, Ray and Eric for showing me what a Man of God looks like.

Most of all I thank my teacher and mentor, Steve Donaldson for showing me what Christ looks like in a man suit.

Persecution 2000:

Preparing the Underground Church

CONTENTS

Persecution 2000:

Preparing the Underground Church

FORWARD:

Three years ago in a city on the South Plains of Texas, God, by His providence brought together a group of people who would impact the nation. These were all Christian warriors, veterans of many campaigns against the strongholds of the enemies of Christ. Among them were seasoned political soldiers, educators, church leaders, medical professionals, military men, Christian apologists, and businessmen. This group crossed denominational barriers, in a unity of purpose only God could produce.

This is a group without membership, without a bank account, without a regular meeting place, but with Christ as the center of every life. There are no appointed "leaders" there, only servants in the pure biblical sense of the word. The Lord has directed them not to become a nonprofit 501-C-3 prisoner to the IRS, and they will take no money from anyone for any reason. They have become a beacon for believers looking for answers to the chaos that has befallen our nation, and the world in these last days. These people are explorers of new territory at the dawn of a new millennium. They are a model for what is bound to become "The Underground Church," in a "post-Christian" America. The name of this group is "Awarehouse." There heart is to evangelize, and stabilize, in other words, "be salt and light.' And their goal is to equip every saint, and set them free to become all that God created them to be.

Awarehouse is a place where a person will learn first to be free in Christ, then to find his individual purpose in God's plan. After that he is equipped and set free upon the enemy under the command of the Holy Spirit alone.

There are many real spiritual heroes at Awarehouse, there

are many called of the Lord as *servant, leaders* who will never be known outside the group, but a few front line soldiers must be point men in the battle. Two of these are Michael Bunker and Steve Donaldson.

Michael and Steve have traveled the country after being invited to appear on numerous radio and television programs to discuss problems, and offer Christ-centered solutions to those problems common to the Christian community in America. They have done many seminars on Christian preparedness, and lectured about the role of the Christian family as God's basic building block for society. They leave no stone left unturned in their presentations as they cover everything from economics to geopolitical strategies, from the persecution of Christians, to the *New World Order's* high-tech attempts to control the masses. They answer questions about everything from Christian self-defense, to how to prepare should there be a breakdown of the societal infrastructure.

The traditional "institutional" safe-havens of *government,* and *church* have generally become bastions of confusion, and bondage during the past few decades in this country, and have left the individual Christian quite helpless in the face of the coming chaos. Michael and Steve have written this book in the hope you find direction to become all He created you to be. And that you find His faithfulness, your purpose, and His will for your life as He makes His house an "Aware-house." "Wait on the Lord and be of good courage, and He shall strengthen thine heart, wait I say on the Lord."

Persecution 2000:

Preparing the Underground Church

"Is not this the fast that I have chosen? to loose the bands of wickedness, to undo the heavy burdens, and to let the oppressed go free, and that ye break every yoke? Is it not to deal thy bread to the hungry, and that thou bring the poor that are cast out to thy house? When thou seest the naked, that thou cover him; and that thou hid not thyself from thine own flesh? Then shall thy light break forth as the morning, and thine health shall spring forth speedily: and thy righteousness shall go before thee; the glory of the Lord shall be thy rereward. Then shall thou call, and the Lord shall answer; thou shalt cry, and he shall say, Here I am. If thou take away from the midst of thee the yoke, the putting forth of the finger, and speaking vanity; And if thou draw out thy soul to the hungry, and satisfy the afflicted soul; then shall thy light rise in obscurity, and thy darkness be as the noonday: And the Lord shall guide thee continually, and satisfy thy soul in drought, and make fat thy bones: and thou shalt be like a watered garden, and like a spring of water, whose waters fail not. And they that shall be of thee shall build the old waste places: thou shalt raise up the foundations of many generations; and thou shalt be called, The repairer of the breach, The restorer of paths to dwell in."

Isaiah 58:6-12

Chapter 1

The Body of Christ
Michael Bunker

"If it meant having no place to lay my head, I knew I must go and tell what I had learned in the camps: That there is no pit so deep or dark that God's love is not deeper still." - Corrie Ten Boom

Blessed are they which are persecuted for righteousness sake: For theirs is the kingdom of heaven." Matthew 5:10 (KJV)

The Manifestation of Persecution

The screams of the Chinese soldiers grew louder as they pounded heavily on the rough pine casket.

"Deny him! Deny him!" They shouted as one of them slowly hammered nails through the coffin lid, sealing it securely with the Christian Pastor inside.

"Deny him!" They shouted, their shouts growing more frantic as the nails were driven home.

Pastor Lee had been warned on four separate occasions against preaching without state approval. On the first occasion, he had been found guilty and sentenced to five years of "reeducation" in a work camp. Every year on the anniversary of his arrival in the prison, he was brought in front of the reeducation tribunal where he was queried about his obstinacy. The first year, the questioning was short and sweet -

"Do you still pray to this Jesus Christ?"

"Yes" he answered.

"Deny him and subscribe to the approved church. You will go free this day".

"I will not."

He was beaten and taken back to his camp.

The second and third years, his captors were much friendlier. They pleaded with him to deny Jesus so they could let him go home. He refused to do so. The next year, he was not even asked. At the end of his fifth year, he was severely beaten and released.

When Pastor Lee returned to his "house church," he found that the number of believers had multiplied. They moved locations constantly - meeting in barns and huts - one week in an apartment above a store on a bustling street, the next week in a copse of trees out in the country.

There were constant brushes with the law. Each week several members of the church volunteered to miss the service so that they could "stand watch," feigning going about their normal business so that they could watch for the authorities, who were constantly searching for "illegal" church meetings.

On the occasion of Pastor Lee's fourth arrest, he was manacled in front of his parishioners. The elders of the church were beaten and arrested as he watched. He was then told that he would deny Christ in front of his church, or he would be buried alive so that the people in front of the church meeting would hear him scream and know that his Jesus could not save him.

Four house church members were conscripted to dig a grave for the pastor while several Chinese policemen unloaded the simple wooden casket from the back of a government truck .

Pastor Lee refused to deny Jesus. He smiled softly as they grabbed him and placed him in the casket. The soldiers became frantic and excited as the nails were driven into the coffin lid. One minute, they were screaming obscenities with hate in their voices, the next they were whimpering, almost pleading with him to relent so that they might free him and go home. He was silent.

After about 40 minutes, they dropped the wooden box in the hole and the order was given to the soldiers to fill the hole in with dirt. Not a sound was heard from inside the casket. The believers were summarily threatened. The "leaders" were carted off to be "reeducated," and a guard was posted at the gravesite for a week.

With the death of Pastor Lee and the incarceration of the house church leadership, the Christian group continues to grow and thrive - and the reeducation camps become training grounds for the next wave of Martyrs in the name of Christ Jesus.

****

Pastor Lee's story is a fictionalized version of actual events, events that happen somewhere in China virtually every day. A persecuted church, driven underground by the forces of evil that reign in the country, is victorious - glorifying JESUS by overcoming. The Chinese Church understands the power of "the blood of the lamb, and the word of their testimony." They are a truly functioning part of the Bride of Christ.

****

In Rwanda, a small nation in central Africa, many of the corpses are still not buried after more than five years - this after the bloody carnage of genocide that swept that tiny nation in 1994. Over 800,000 Rwandese (predominately Tutsi and Christian) were murdered in less than 100 days. This was not accomplished by an organized and efficient "assembly line" process by a small portion of the population, but, for the most part, by consensus of

13

over 80% of the population armed with machetes and a firm desire to wipe the Tutsi Christian off the map.

Such barbarism, not seen since the crusades, was possible in part because of the assistance and collaboration of the Christian Church leadership in the nation.

"What?!?"

"Surely not," you say.

In many of the documented cases of mass murder during this disaster, entire Christian church bodies were slaughtered after their "leadership" handed them over for massacre by the *genocidaires* (those who commit genocide). This phenomenal event was chronicled in the recently released book, We Wish To Inform You, That Tomorrow We Will Be Killed With Our Families, by author and researcher Philip Gourevitch. The chilling title of the book came from a letter given by the pastors in a community to their church president, a Hutu. The church president then turned over the letter to the genocidaires who promptly slaughtered the faithful group of believers the following day. The church president felt validated in his decision, and a few years later was quoted as saying that what he had done was alright. After all, if he had not turned his sheep over to be massacred, the killers would still have murdered them all; only his own body, and that of his wife would have been included in the number.

The bodies of Christian believers are still piled up like cord wood in many of the churches in Rwanda - a ghastly memorial to failed leadership and headship in a dark world, growing darker day by day.

****

The contrast in leadership between these two stories is stark; but the contrast brings into focus a worldwide event, (that has been a nonevent in the media and the halls of power) that is, the unprecedented persecution of the Body of Christ in the world today, and the unmistakable message it brings to those who sit blindly in the plush pews of the American organized church.

****

That Christians at the end of the 20th century would be persecuted, is not altogether a shock. It is clear in the prophetic scriptures that, as time goes by, those who are in darkness will increasingly rail against the light. The "accuser of the brethren" has now had all of two millennia to establish the world views and other human mechanisms that would assist such persecution. We must realize, however, that Christianity is designed for it; after all, Christians serve "another King." They are by definition, outsiders - ambassadors from a strange place that has neither space nor time. Christian believers are not subject to the powers and principalities of this world. We are supposed to be separate and unequal. Our standard operating procedure is to function according to the commands of a Spirit which others can neither see nor hear. Our Master delights in confounding the wisdom of the wise - He chooses broken vessels in which to carry His message. He validates His word by showing that he is "hyper-dimensional," that He operates outside of our known dimensions.

We are the perfect candidates for persecution. We are ideally suited to be carried before kings and rulers as treasonous terrorists, insane malefactors, and dangerous traitors primed to lead a revolt against tyrannical human authority.

A born-again believer is capable of withstanding debasement, torture and ridicule in order to steadfastly glorify his King. He is designed to fight valiantly, withstand courageously, overcome gloriously, and die honorably. Paul Marshall wrote in his landmark book, Their Blood Cries Out, Christians *"embody a loyalty to a standard of spiritual allegiance apart from the political order. This fact itself denies that the state is the all encompassing or ultimate arbiter of human life. Regardless of how the relationship between God and Caesar has been expressed, it now at least means that, contra the Romans and modern totalitarians, Caesar is not God. This confession, however mute, sticks in the craw of every authoritarian regime and draws their angry and bloody response.*

"Many Christians are therefore persecuted simply because they are Christians. Their usually peaceful and quiet beliefs stand as a rebuke to those who are corrupt, to those who cannot tolerate the presence of any view but their own, and to those who want to make their own political regime the focus of loyalty. Their very existence is a silent witness to a claim beyond human control."

Caesar is not GOD! We are not subject to his godlessness either. Those leaders in the organized church who place believers under the subjection of lawless rulers are doing violence to the body of Christ. The Bible says that he who has authority is a ruler who punishes evil and rewards good. Why is it that church leaders will command the brethren to obey those who punish good and reward evil? Have we come to the time in history when wolves, entering into the sheepfold are calling good/evil and evil/good? The book of third John teaches us well in this regard. In chapter eleven of that book it states, *"Beloved, follow not that which is evil, but that which is good. He that doeth evil hath not seen GOD. "* (KJV)

The Christian believer, in doing well, rejects evil leadership - subscribing all the while to the Kingship of Jesus Christ alone. In doing so, he is guaranteed the wrath of despotic tyrants.

So why, then, has the American Church suffered so little?

The answer is embodied in the premise of the question. Either we have subjected ourselves to unholy leadership and paid alms to Caesar (In which case we are rewarded with the long, healthy lives of cowards), or we actually do have righteous leadership - and therefore are not under an obligation to resist. If the reader chooses the latter of the two options, then the time you spent reading this book will be wasted. Under righteous leadership there is no need for an underground church, or for martyrs. If, however, you find the first response to be uncomfortable, but true - then we can be certain of three things:

1. The judgment of GOD is sure.
2. Those who resist Caesar, will be punished.
3. Those who wish to live Holy (separate unto Him, for His

purpose) in Christ Jesus, WILL suffer persecution.

"Blessed are ye, when men shall revile you, and persecute you, and shall say all manner of evil against you falsely, for my sake. Rejoice and be exceeding glad: for great is your reward in heaven: for so persecuted they the prophets which were before you."
Matthew 5:11-12 (KJV)

****

"Courage is not simply one of the virtues, but the form of every virtue at it's testing point, which means, at the point of highest reality. A chastity or honesty or mercy which yields to danger will be chaste or honest or merciful only on conditions. Pilate was merciful 'till it became risky." C.S. Lewis, The Screwtape Letters

One of the biggest challenges facing the Body of Christ in America at the turn of the millennium, is the complete and utter failure of Christian leadership. We will go into some of the reasons behind that failure in the next chapter; but for now we will discuss the nature of the error in which this "leadership" has entangled us.

In the last several American elections, Christian leaders have rallied the troops like never before. Activists pounded the streets and swarmed the polling places in numbers never before seen in the history of American politics. The standard podium pounding motivational speech led many to believe that if they worked hard enough, volunteered often enough, and prayed devoutly enough - they could actually elect the Messiah and "fix" the mess into which we have worked ourselves. Christians piled their prayers into politics and party - pardoning themselves for their lack of attention to the spiritual health of their communities and, more importantly, their families. While the "wins" stacked up on election night, those who had eyes to see and ears to hear, noticed

17

that divorce rates among Christians had come to equal that of the secular world, and more and more of the children of the Promise were being placed into the custody of Child Welfare and Juvenile Detention authorities.

Once again, the Children of GOD were forsaking their master and demanding an earthly "king" to come and fix it all.

****

Another ghastly error reared its ugly head while Christians in America were becoming politically active. A large portion of the Church succumbed to what I can only call Prosperity Teaching. In untold numbers, pastors roped people into their churches and "revivals" with promises of riches and glory. During a time when the Body of Christ worldwide was suffering the greatest persecution in its history - American churches were throwing MILLIONS of dollars at building contractors with the hope of seducing the richest and most consistent tithers into their churches. Their palaces of iniquity grew more and more ornate as the bodies of the brethren piled up in Rwanda and the Sudan and elsewhere in the world.

As three hundred million believers were being tortured, killed, raped and imprisoned for their faith - American churches bought carpet and windows and doors and buildings to house the vast numbers of people being "saved" each week. This is not to say that people were not reached for Jesus Christ, nor is it to say that Churches should not have carpet and windows. What it does say, is that a large number of churches refused to report on "the state of the Body," so that church members would not limit their giving to the corporation.

In late 1998 while travelling to an expo in Denver, Colorado, I was interviewed by a Christian radio host who was doing a show about "revival" in America. Pastors had been calling in for over an hour, telling glowing stories of the "revival" in their churches. It seemed like the whole nation was getting "saved".

The talk show host asked me if I believed there was going to be a nationwide revival in America. "I mean a pouring out of the

Holy Spirit from the President to the dogcatcher?," he asked.

I laughed a bit, then replied, "Absolutely not."

He seemed surprised for a second, then asked "Why not?"

I said, "Name one post-Christian nation in history which has turned back to GOD in repentance and returned to its former glory."

He stumbled for a minute, then asked me what I did think was going to happen.

"It's quite easy," I said, "to get ten thousand people to show up to a service and get "saved" when you promise them money and fame and prosperity. My question to you is, could you get ten-thousand people to show up if you preached to them of the offense of the Cross, the cost of discipleship, the expense (to Christ) of propitiation? When you preach True freedom purchased by blood sacrifice on a rugged wooden Cross, only those who understand that cost, admit their need, and submit to the Spirit, will come."

How many preachers are teaching suffering, like the Reformers preached? How many preachers are setting their flocks free from bondage?

"The problem," I told the host, "Is a misunderstanding of the word "revival." We think revival is when we throw up a sign - or a tent; or when a large number of people get "saved" in a short amount of time. But revival literally means "RE-LIFE." To have revival, you have to have had LIFE in the first place. Dead sinners being given life by Christ is NOT revival - It is SALVATION!

Revival is when a malfunctioning part of the body, convicted of error, repents of that error and submits itself to the Head. For example, if the hand is in error, disobeys the Head and touches a hot stove - it suffers from its disobedience. It is not disowned by the Head, it is still a hand and it is still part of the body; it is just in error and is subject to the temporal physical punishment of disobedience. Now, if the hand "repents" and turns away from the stove - it is spared the suffering and injury of disobedience and, in full submission to the Head, has JOY as a submissive part of the Body. This is revival. The hand enjoys LIFE-AGAIN or "Re-life" as a functioning and efficient part of the body.

****

Mary, an Egyptian Christian, tells her story slowly. There is pain in her voice. She was kidnapped by Muslim fanatics in late 1997. She was tortured and raped repeatedly for months. Acid was poured on her wrists, disfiguring her so as to obliterate crosses that she had tattooed on her arms to show her allegiance to Christ.

When Mary's father contacted the police, he was told not to interfere with her "conversion" to Islam - and that he was not to look for her or make any trouble. When her captors threatened to destroy her face permanently - she reluctantly agreed to convert to Islam.

Mary escaped months later. She reconverted to Christianity, and now leads her life in hiding. Her son lives with her. He is a product of the brutal rapes she endured while in captivity.

Mary's experience is repeated daily throughout the Muslim world - she is an example of the brutal persecution faced by the children of God at the hands of evil men, who in doing so, persecute Christ.

Mary had faith that Christ was with her while she was being brutalized. She knows He is with her now in her hiding place. It seems that today, there is a misunderstanding of the word "faith," and how it applies to the believer.

****

About a year ago, we (Steve Donaldson and I) were accused publicly by a television preacher of having "no faith," because we were encouraging believers to get prepared for the troubles that are surely coming. The preacher did not deny that troubles were coming. He did not deny that we are in desperate shape in this country. But still he challenged our faith.

The television preacher scoffed at us, called us names and told his audience to do NOTHING to prepare for themselves or others in the days to come. To do ANYTHING, he claimed, would show a lack of faith in GOD. "God will miraculously save us," he said.

This preacher, in insisting on a miracle from God, was denying that we ALREADY POSSESS a miracle! We live in a country where it costs us nothing to believe - where there is little persecution, and the average believer can choose between twenty different churches to attend, all within driving distance of his home.

Instead, this preacher, and many others like him - shake a bony finger in the face of God, demanding further miracles so that he might save us from our complacency, and repay us for our powerful "faith." This is offensive on its face. Christ has provided us with uncountable miracles. We are a prosperous, wealthy and decadent church. We are likely the Laodecian church of the last days - our most notable quality is our luke warmness, and each day that this country is not destroyed by Almighty God for its iniquity, is a gift from God himself - a gift with which He exhibits his Grace towards us, and His longsuffering.

"For what glory is it, if, when ye be buffeted for your faults, ye shall take it patiently? But if, when ye do well, and suffer for it, ye take it patiently, this is acceptable with GOD". 1 Peter 2:20

"Find out just what any people will quietly submit to, and you have found the exact measure of injustice and wrong which will be imposed upon them." -Frederick Douglass

****

I recently listened to a speech by General Ed Wheeler who was discussing the tactics used to plan the Gulf War. He made an interesting statement. He said, "An army NEVER makes its plans based on an adversaries intentions. Intentions can change overnight. An army ALWAYS makes its strategic plans based on an enemies capabilities. Intentions change rapidly, capabilities do not."

This quote struck me as an extremely wise one. How does

it apply to us, the Body of Christ - the Army of God?

We have staked our lives, and those of our families, on the stated intentions of a growing authoritarian state. Never mind that the evil one has slowly, through time, set in place the mechanisms by which we can be killed or enslaved. We have, for the most part, rejected the idea that our enemies will make use of these evil capabilities - and we have been sold a bill of goods based on "good intentions".

While our government will have us believe that they have "granted" us freedom of worship, they have also built dozens of civilian internment camps. Many of the executive orders (eo's) and Presidential Decision Directives that authorized this are available on the internet for your perusal. Their intentions for these camps are immaterial - intentions can change. While they will have us believe that they have "granted" us amnesty from taxation, they have provided the mechanism by which they can terrorize and threaten the incorporated church. Ask your pastor if there is not the implied threat that political speech will not be tolerated in the incorporated church. The stated intention to provide tax-free status is a ruse devised by the enemy to prevent moral authorities in the Body of Christ from speaking out against the evil capabilities of government. The mere hint that tax authorities are looking into "violations" in a church is enough to frighten away the average church member and intimidate the pastor into compliance. That these churches have submitted to this charlatanism and witchcraft on the part of government, is the measure of our failure as leaders and as believers in Christ. The organized church has willfully or ignorantly submitted themselves to despots, and in an unmistakable way, have declared, "We have no King, but Caesar!"

****

One of the most interesting things I have noticed as I travel the country speaking to churches and Christian groups - is the profound distrust that many people, believers in particular, have for their government. This distrust is manifested in an overwhelming feeling of fear. Fear that "speaking out" or even meeting to discuss

22

issues important to the Body of Christ will get one "placed on a list" somewhere. I have had Christian believers tell me that they will not even attend a bible study where politics or socio-political events are discussed, for fear that someone there is an informer, or that someone will be out in the parking lot writing down license plate numbers. Unfortunately - these feelings are often justified.

When someone as respected in the Christian community as Dr. James Dobson of Focus On The Family, can be linked to a "hate crime" (by NBC's Katie Couric and homosexual advocates) something is wrong. Couric attacked Dobson on television because he openly supported television and print advertisements that portray homosexuality as a poor life-style choice that can be overcome. It seems we have a situation that is not unlike that which was created in 1930's Nazi Germany, or in early 1990's Rwanda, where an entire segment of the population is painted as the "enemy" of progressivism in the nation. History teaches us that this is a slippery slope that leads to the scapegoatism of perceived enemies to "social progress." The very existence of these enemies threaten the social order that the corrupt forces dream of enacting in the nation.

Martin Niemoller, Deidrich Boenhoffer and many other Christian martyrs who were put to death by the Nazi's during World War II, wrote of identical situations and feelings prior to the rise of National Socialism in Germany. Irrational accusations and widespread public scapegoatism in the media were telltale signs of the oppression and persecution that was to come for the Jews, the Gypsies, and even European Christians of that time. Open up a Pakastani, Sudanese or Egyptian newspaper today and you will read "opinion" columns which call Jews and Christians cannibals who are "subhuman" blasphemers who are enemies of Allah. Many Muslim children are taught that to kill a Christian or a Jew is fulfilling the wishes of God, and will earn one a place in "paradise".

PLO Chairman Yasser Arafat is often seen speaking in public with signs behind him that read in arabic "WE WILL KILL THE JEWS ON SATURDAY (their sabbath), AND THE CHRISTIANS ON SUNDAY." This seemingly absurd statement is a main tenet of the PLO charter, and is as ingrained in the teachings of Palestinian youth as the pledge of allegiance is to many Americans.

Our national government has, since 1993, participated with the enemies of Israel in the partition and division of the Holy Land that GOD himself gave to the Children of Israel. Our executive branch has legitimized the terrorist Muslim authority of the PLO and of many other middle eastern administrations, and has played the roll of Ad-Man and PR guru for the terrorist Arafat himself.

Are we to believe that nobody in the State Department speaks or reads Arabic? Or is it more likely that those in authority in America today share in the Palestinian goal of the destruction of the Jewish race and the subsequent murder and persecution of Christians?

****

So what is the big deal? So there are people who don't like us. So we have some dumb leadership, why make such a big deal out of it? The stories and facts put forth in this first chapter were designed to be like a history primer/news update that gives you a big picture of where we are on GOD's time line. If we were able to separate ourselves from our 3D world for a minute and look at the world from GOD's perspective, we would see how the powers and principalities of this age are conspiring to bring about the death and destruction of the people of GOD. Now, that is not to say that GOD is not in charge - He certainly is - it is only to point out that we very well may be entering into a time in history, about which the Bible says more than any other time, including the time in which Jesus of Nazareth walked the streets of Judea. Much of the Bible is an exhortation to the people of GOD to be strong in times of trouble. Much of it is a lesson in denying SELF and relying on Him to work in us that which will allow us to overcome in times of persecution. Many of the giants of the faith have been tortured and killed for their testimony, and right now MILLIONS of believers are enduring the same fate. So the questions arise - Why is America different? Why have we been spared (thus far) the same fate as Christians the world over? Why will the Body of Christ in America not hear the warnings and prayerful exhortations of those in bondage that we are steamrolling towards the same fate? Are we really so prideful that we believe that our faith is stronger than that of the believers in the Sudan (1.5 million murdered), or in Rwanda (800,000 slaughtered), or in China (uncountable numbers in prison camps, murdered, tortured)?

Is persecution coming to America? How do we survive and thrive under the coming persecution? What lessons can we learn from those who have endured oppression in the past? What is it that is broken in the American church that needs to be analyzed and faced in order for us to understand why persecution is inevitable? We will examine the root of these questions in the next chapter, however it is necessary at this juncture, to point out for you the primary reason that there is now a growing need for a spirit driven, fully functioning, persecution proof UNDERGROUND CHURCH. What is this reason? THE RISE OF ANTI-CHRISTIANITY

Our good friend and colleague S.G. Smith defined anti-Christianity well in his brilliant 1996 book entitled Origins of Destiny: The Heritage of Nations:

"Aside from our obvious fleshly sins, the constant cultural brainwashing of misinformation presses us toward a global regime of anti-Christianity. What are the means which must be implemented to achieve these goals?"

Corresponding to the divine institutions, they may be summarized as follows:

1. Labor, wealth, and property must be confiscated, regulated, or controlled to constrain people to comply with any desired anti-Christian agenda.
2. Marriage may need to be limited, regulated, or married life subverted in order to direct the energies of a couple toward areas other than marital union.
3. Family life must be replaced and broadened within the context of a different group so that youth absorb a community concept alien or adverse to normal family unity and authority.

4. The philosophy of government must be redefined, broadened by force of law, and redirected into areas other than executing capital offenses and maintaining civil order.

5. Local governments, nations, and ethnic groups must be uniformly amalgamated in order to achieve a level of global compliance consistent with the above.

6. Physical and "spiritual" Israel must be absorbed, neutralized, or eliminated since they pose a constant threat to any anti-Christian agenda.

Smith goes on to say, "As opposed to insuring divine endowments of life, liberty and the pursuit of happiness (which primarily implied property), an anti-Christian framework must seek to disenfranchise citizens of life, liberty, and property."

"It might be noted that various religious cults have often learned how to implement the first three points. National governments of course, provide a broader platform in which to develop the full agenda. When this finally happens, this so called one world government will in fact be a one world cult."

"I have begun to understand that human beings can be made to believe that black is white if they are fed enough mental doses of gray over long periods of time. And I have learned that anyone who trusts his property to a banker, his liberty to a lawyer or his life to a medical doctor is very, very foolish. . . and the biggest fool of all is he who would trust his soul to a preacher." — J. Patrick Shannan I Rode With Tupper, Founders Publishing Co. 1992. Pg. 205.

****

Many Christian leaders now believe that America is no longer a "post-Christian nation", but that we have become an "anti-Christian nation". How did this come about? How has the one world cult come to soil the greatest Christian nation on the face of the planet? We'll examine that in the next chapter.

Chapter 2

A Bride in Tattered Garments
Steve Donaldson

His watchmen are blind: they are all ignorant, they are all dumb dogs, they cannot bark; sleeping, lying down, loving to slumber. Yea, they are greedy dogs which can never have enough, and they are shepherds that cannot understand: they all look to their own way, every one for his gain, from his quarter.
(Isaiah 56:10-11)
Therefore shall evil come upon thee; thou shalt not know from whence it riseth: and mischief shall fall upon thee; thou shalt not be able to put it off: and desolation shall come upon thee suddenly, which thou shalt not know.
(Isaiah 47:11)

The Result

Tears rolled down her cheeks and the words barely escaped trembling lips, as the woman I will call Amy described the chaos which now characterizes her family – a family which had been well known in its community as a "wonderful Christian family..."

I am a Christian teacher and counselor, and for many years I've sat with too many "Amys." There are too many like her, and the problems are getting worse. Not only are problems like Amy's becoming more commonplace, but the entire nation seems to be falling apart in lock-step with the Christian family. Is there a common denominator? Is there a linkage between the condition of the Christian family and the destiny of nations? As I prayerfully considered these questions, the answers became crystal clear. I was horrified when I realized "I" had become a part of the problem! But who knows, as we proceed to the root of the problem, you may discover some personal culpability also. Your destiny, that of your family, and in turn the destinies of your community and our nation may well rest upon your response to what will be put forth here in the next few pages. .

Time is very short. We are about to see families like Amy's and our nation, with all its "institutions," either find "right" answers or be destroyed. Amy's family problems are a microcosm of the problems faced by the Church as an "institution" and those of our nation as a whole. Since nations are made of families and the family is "ordained" by God as the basic building block of His Church, Christian families should exhibit His character to the world. They should also be the world's model for unity, stability, and godly character. So what happened?

The Body of Christ in this country is floundering. We are broken as a Body. We are fragmented, seemingly powerless, and quite frankly, we don't look much different from the "walking dead" out there in the world. We are NOT the cultural model we are supposed to be. We have become a laughing stock to the whole world.

We pray for revival, yet we suffer apathy. We plan community and political action, but the abortion rate keeps climbing and our political leaders become more decadent. From Home Groups to Promise Keepers, we plan and work and the only products we see are tired, frustrated Christians. The Bride seems even more desperately ill than the society she was sent to rescue. Is this a part of His plan? Does it fit into prophecy? What are we supposed to know? What are we supposed to do? What are we supposed to be like in this place and in this time? How did this Bride of Christ in the United States of America come to this? The questions just keep coming.

A Caveat

I need to offer a word of caution at this point. What follows in these pages may violate your comfort zone. This is going to be a discussion about the corporate Church as it is seen today and is an observation of the state of the Body as a whole. It is also an exploration into the ways individual believers should act in order to be responsible "Body parts" during these last days. I believe one, and perhaps *the* most important, way individuals should structure their behavior is based on the hierarchies God has set up within Creation He has ordained a certain order to serve as the model for right behavior for the individual and for right relationships between individuals; and He has placed certain people to function as leaders of certain groups so that things will function rightly.

But before we talk about these models and the hierarchies God has set up, let me make a few things clear at the outset. God has ordained an order for things which enables them to function rightly, and this order of things works in conjunction with, not in conflict to, our position before Him as individual believer-priests. Each believer, whether male or female, married or single, is called to a priesthood in this world for our King Jesus. We each stand alone in accountability before Him, with Jesus as our sole Mediator. No human stands between the believer-priest and God. And because His Son has paid the price for our sins with His life, we can approach God as our Father, our Friend, and our Counselor with boldness. We now have the privilege of being alone with Him on an individual basis. And with Christ in *us* as our only hope of glory, we are partakers of the mind of Christ. We all have the same anointing and have no need that anyone should teach us.

So, the object of this discussion is not so much to teach, but rather to destroy an errant modern paradigm. It is intended to call your attention away from the noise of the world so that you, the believer, will stop to listen for His voice and respond accordingly.

The Turning

Because we are ultimately accountable to God as individuals, we need to look at some of the things which affect our relationship with Him. One thing which stands out as a factor which can affect our daily relationship with our Father is what is commonly known as *repentance*. This is a subject raised throughout scripture; and as one studies the subject, it becomes obvious repentance is a continual process for the believer. It is a constant turning from *wrongheadedness*. That is a mouthful, but it expresses the concept beautifully. Repentance involves a turning away from wrong thinking and its fruit, wrong behavior. If we do not turn from our wrong thinking, we will reap a terrible crop in the coming years. So, how does one repent? *It is the goodness of God that leads to repentance* (Romans 2:4.) What is the goodness of God that leads to repentance? Well, often it does not appear as "goodness," and it is simply pride that keeps us from seeing it as His goodness.

Pride is that mind-set that comes when a person is unable to see God "rightly;" rather he sees God, the world, and himself through his own eyes and lives accordingly. Pride won't let us see the goodness of God; therefore, there can be no turning. Pride prompts us to continue down traditional and familiar paths to misery and ineffectiveness. Pride also leads to compromise with the world, compelling us to take worldly tactics when we do battle with the world and its systems. Paul has rightly said, *We do not wrestle against flesh and blood...* (Ephesians 6:12) It is time for a change. It is time for us to abandon that pride which puts a wedge between us and our Creator in our daily communing with one another. It is time for us to become humble.

Humility is that mind-set which comes when a person is able to see God, the world, and himself through the eyes of God and live accordingly. Humility brings peace of mind; it brings rest into worlds filled with chaos. Where is that peace and rest to which we are called? It is hidden from us by our own eyes! We are flailing because our pride keeps us from looking at the gospel of Jesus Christ and His instruction through humility. Instead, we run to any perverted or incomplete concepts of His Gospel and Truth as a quick fix to our problems. We stay in our wrongheadedness.

So as we explore the way believers are supposed to live in this world and the mind-set they should adopt in the living of the adventure, by God's grace our eyes will be opened to seeing His goodness. And in this process, one of the first things we will see as we look at His goodness, is our own wretchedness. But in looking at our wretchedness and recognizing we have a problem, we've already taken the first step toward the solution. According to the riches of His grace, may He allow us to see rightly. Now, let's take a look.

A Picture of Deception

We wrestle not against flesh and blood... (Ephesians 6:12) So what is the origin of our problems? If you were to ask yourself who would profit most from the Bride being "tattered," who do you think it might be? Let's drift for a moment into the worlds of Peretti and Lewis and observe a dialogue of the type which might remind you of *Screwtape* and *Wormwood*. This is a world outside our space-time continuum in "Somewhere-time." Let's listen to this conversation between Satan and one of his henchmen, and maybe we can grab a clue...

"I will have this world! I'll show Him! I'll consume all He's made, all He holds dear!" Satan paced about in anger, shaking his fist in the air.

"But how will you do it, Most Evil Master? We control most of the earthly kingdoms, but there is yet one kingdom in our way. It is the most powerful one ever. It is founded by followers of our enemy Jesus. They follow Him faithfully, they prosper, they send His Word all over the world. We'll never be able to gain it all with *them* in power!"

"Ahh, but I have a delicious defeat in store for them."

"What is it, Most Evil One? Is it enticing them into New Age religion? Is it economic catastrophes? Is it the devastation of war? Maybe it could be the destruction caused by drugs! Is it apathy? Tell me what it is! How are we going to gain your New World

Order?"

"It is not any of those. Indeed, my plan will cause all of that; but it's much simpler and more beautiful than *just* those few things. The plan is simple, and... oh, so easy! In order for us to gain our New World Order, the United States must go down. Right?"

"Right, Your Evilness. But we know America's strength comes from the Christian Church. How can we defeat America when His Church is so strong?"

"You are correct. So ... that 'Bride of Christ' must go down. Defeat the Church in the United States, and we have our New World Order."

"Great Father of Lies, how do we accomplish that? Do we begin with persecution?"

"No, no, no!" screamed Satan, "That never works. Haven't you seen how they grow stronger in persecution? We have to avoid that martyr stuff at all costs! No! Let them have their time with flesh work. Keep them nice and comfortable. Keep them out of the real fight. And when we see someone who is in the fight, we must concentrate our attack there. We have to hit the main ones, the leaders."

"Oh, I see.... it's the preachers who must go down! It's the preachers and elders and deacons . . . now, I see!"

"NO again! It's not those guys! They were never intended to be the *real* leaders. We have to leave them alone. They are actually an asset to us right now. Their roles have become so polluted that they have become essential to our goal of achieving our New World Order."

"What? Who do we hit, then, Evil Master?"

"It's the men, you dote! It's the husbands, the fathers, and brothers who were intended to lead His Bride into the promised land! Destroy the role of the Christian male in America as the servant of his family, and the 'Bride' will fall, the nation will fall, and then everything will fall into our hands! The only thing left standing will be shallow, powerless institutions. And controlling institutions is my speciality!"

"So, the first thing we must do is to take out those men out who pose a real threat. Their Master has rightly told them, *And whosoever will be chief among you, let him be your servant: Even as the Son of man came not to be ministered unto, but to minister, and to give his life a ransom for many.* (Matthew 20:27-28) Once we remove the men from their God-ordained servant role as 'Prophet, Priest and King' of their families, they will automatically lose their role as the family *leader*. Whoever or *whatever* serves the family as Prophet, Priest and King will be their leader by default. Our job will be accomplished by making *something else* the leader. Then our warrior, General Confusion, can begin his work."

"What, Sir, is so important about their men being 'Prophet,' 'Priest,' and 'King?'

"Don't you see? The Creator designed the system perfectly. It was designed to reflect His glory and to enable man to relate to Him. Even though it was broken through the Fall, He had designed the perfect solution in the sacrifice of His son... enabling them to become like Christ. The model He created is perfect.

Each of the parts, the 'Prophet,' the 'Priest,' and the 'King' play a role in accomplishing that perfect model within Creation. The 'Prophet' is to bring a proper word at a proper time. He is one to whom a person goes for answers to problems of living and for counsel, encouragement, and instruction. People rely upon the 'Prophet' to help keep them from error and repair relationships. The 'Prophet' is a servant: people depend upon servants, they follow servants. If they can be fooled into following the wrong 'Prophet,' they can be fed all kinds of information full of lies and half-truths. They will begin to lose respect for the ones whom God designed to be 'Prophets.' Husbands, dads, and brothers will begin to look like ignorant fools who can't be trusted. Their relationships will begin to deteriorate, and families in chaos will be a sweet result for us."

"That's wonderful, Great Wizard of Woe, but what about the role of 'Priest?' Aren't they all 'Priests' individually anyway? What's the big deal?"

"Okay, Maggot, here's the real issue. This family 'Priest' doesn't stand between anyone and God. You know that. But this 'Priest' is both special and vital to the Creator's purpose. He stands as a metaphor for God in society. He is the one to be trusted with responsibilities, looked to for answers, and relied upon in times of crisis. It is his duty to model the way humans are to conduct themselves before God. The family Priest preserves unity, not only in the family, but for society in general. Unity is a very big thing with the Creator.

When his children see him go to God with his problems, he is teaching by his conduct. They learn they can also go directly to God with their problems. We don't want that, do we? We want them to go to the "institution" so we can have our fun with them. The 'Priest' is the one who teaches about God, models Christ-likeness. It is the 'Priest' to whom they go for instruction on how to 'hear God's voice,' how to pray, and how to understand His Word. It is the 'Priest' who instructs them about communication with God.

If we persuade them to follow *something* or someone, *anything* or anyone but the God-ordained family leader, then we will get some interesting results. We will find them depending upon *something*, or someone, that may or may not be telling them the TRUTH about God and His plan of redemption. They can easily be fooled into thinking He doesn't really hold them so securely. Our Colonels, Doubt and Fear, can then rule in their hearts. When that happens, they can be easily convinced that the Cross of Christ *alone* isn't sufficient for their salvation. Once they are fed that little morsel, they are vulnerable to General Guilt and his demonic horde. They will begin to do all kinds of 'busy work' trying to gain His approval. They will start feeling superior to others because of how much work they do *for the Lord*, or they will feel inferior because they aren't doing enough. They will become spiritually depressed or religious and mean spirited; either way is good for our plan.

Then there is the 'King' role. Ah... it is a thing of beauty when properly destroyed! Just as He set up the 'Prophet' and 'Priest' as special roles for this servant-ruler, He also set up the 'King' to be provider, and protector-defender of the family. He is the one who sets the standards for right behavior. And as 'King,' he is the one who keeps them safe from me. But a 'King' who doesn't have the respect of his subjects is really no 'King' at all, is he? When this *supposed* 'King' abdicates his authority and hands it off to the

34

'hired ones' of the 'institution' (that *something* I was referring to earlier), he becomes nothing more than a confused dictator who spends all his time putting out the fires of life, dumping his confusion on everyone around him. He is functionally out of the fight. He has moved from servant-leader to helpless follower. When he tries to set standards, they will question his every move because he has no real authority, no reference point, and little or no personal knowledge of the way God designed things to work. They will not trust him to protect and defend them because they will see their lives in chaos and recognize it is the result of his lack of leadership. In turn, they will be in a constant state of lack; they will be needy. Their neediness is good for us too. He is reduced only to the role of 'provider' and will find it an empty, lonely place where no one really understands him. Oh, he can be really proud of all his efforts and accomplishments at 'work,' but he will keep his mouth shut at home to save face. The result is marvelous! He is emasculated! And in the process of keeping his mouth shut, he will wind up killing the very relationships he has been commissioned to nurture.

What a wonderfully sad monarch he's become. He is disrespected, even hated, because they all know he is supposed to be trustworthy and responsible; however, he has become anything *but* that. He is supposed to know how life is to be lived and teach them the principles God laid down; but instead, he sends them off to a 'surrogate' Prophet, Priest, and King for instructions about life. He sends them off to the 'institution' for instruction and guidance.

Now that we have stripped this king, he is standing naked in his lonely mansion screaming into the darkness, 'I am the authority here...Where is the submission? You are supposed to submit and obey....I am the king, won't somebody listen to me! I am the king, where is my respect, where is my family! Oh! My God, my God! I've done my part, why won't they listen!!'

The hierarchy is now broken! The basic building block of the Body of Christ, the family, is now destroyed. We have accomplished dependency upon the 'hired ones' and the 'institutions,' and now we have them right where we want them. They are totally dependent upon us.

Now we can bring crisis upon His creation and put our New World Order in place. Since we control the 'institution' by neatly hobbling them with government rule and muzzling the 'hired ones' by laws, the families will actually be running to me for safety! There is no nucleus to hold them together. They will see no option but to run to *my* minions, now! They will beg me to lead them! I, Lucifer, will not only control their rightful corporate Prophet, Priest, and King; *I* will become their *appointed* prophet, priest, and king. Just imagine the joy of it: His people worshiping at the feet of the god of this world!

The thing that makes it even sweeter is that our Enemy, the Great Creator, has tried to warn them of our plan, but they weren't able to hear. *As for my people, children are their oppressors, and women rule over them. O my people, they which lead thee cause thee to err, and destroy the way of thy paths.* (Isaiah 3:12) Their tenderly tickled ears became deaf with apathy and their eyes became blinded by comfort. They gladly relinquished their responsibilities. Now we can pick them off one at a time until we've torn all the garments off His 'Bride.' The man will be destroyed, the family will be in chaos, the United States will be falling as the New World Order becomes a reality!"

"Evil Master of Misery, that is beautiful! It is such a wonderful plan, and extremely easy to work. They all think they are doing what they are *supposed* to do and all the time they are playing right into your most unholy hands. Let the destruction begin........."

The Purpose and the Design

I hope the conversation above was enough to clue you into the reason we find this Bride in such tattered garments. I am not one who likes to dwell upon problems; I'd rather move through to solutions. But in this case, a complete understanding of the problem is a necessary part of the solution. Why would a person return again and again to the same Physician when the illness gets worse with every prescription he's given? That's what we seem to be doing in America today, especially within the "church."

After many years of seeing this Body and this country sink together into what looks a great deal like the end times *Babylon*, I realized the mechanisms of "church" and "government" must not be working the way the Creator intended. You see, if the design for something is proper and the use of it is right, then the results are always going to be a thing of precision and beauty. But the chaotic results we see in the church and the government today betray errant design or improper usage.

Let me give you an example of what I mean. When we watch the launch of a space shuttle, it is a thing of beauty. But it wasn't always like that. I remember back in the '60s when we were involved in the "space race" with the old Soviet Union. We had far more failures than successes with our rockets until the design engineers finally got it right. All those failures were the result of wrongheadedness on the part of the designers. They didn't know everything they needed to know to make it work right. But, as their ideas came into alignment with the truth about the "laws" of aerodynamics, the "laws" of physics, and the other "laws" of science, they became more successful with each new project. As they found the truth within the universe that applies to rockets and thrusters and gravitational forces and all the other minutia involved in launching hundreds of tons of metal out of the earth's grip, they finally achieved their goal. They put a man on the moon!

Our space program is now far more beautiful in its working than anyone could have imagined, but it is so only because we have more knowledge of truth from within the universe and have the wisdom to follow that truth. The disasters happened because we *thought* we were right when we *thought* it was designed according to the "laws" of physics and we *thought* we were using it right.

This point is illustrated daily in all our lives and is often expressed in words like: "Man, that should have worked or "I sure thought I had it fixed this time" or "If I'd only known then what I know now." And then there is my all time favorite, "Come to think of it, that was kinda stupid wasn't it?" What we observe here is people who think they know "truth" and think they are operating by its principles; yet, they are continually surrounded by chaos.

Because they are in chaos, it is obvious they are not operating according to "truth." Instead, they suffer from making wrong assumptions about the purpose for which they were made and wrong assumptions about how they were designed by their Creator to achieve that purpose. Confusion and chaos are always the result of making wrong assumptions about God and His purpose for His creation. There is "truth" in creation that must be followed if things are going to function properly. But before I go on, I want to make a few brief observations about purpose, design, and the success that comes with proper usage of God's created order.

Wrong purposes get wrong results. Purpose always begins with a desire or a need. Human beings are found, more often than not, pursuing false needs. An example of this can be seen in a statement like: "We need more people in church, so let's get the best preacher we can find and get the very best teachers in town." The statement betrays an errant purpose. We may come up with a great design for this false purpose; but in so doing, we miss the real intent for His preachers and their "flock." We miss our real purpose as a Body and create false dependencies. It is Christ alone who will build His Church. He designed the system so that the really important teaching and bonding of the Body begins in the home. The purpose for the 'Christ-built' church is to make His manifold wisdom known to the powers and principalities in the heavenly realms. In other words, our purpose is to show angels and demons the multifaceted wisdom of God as we acknowledge and serve Him.

As we acknowledge and serve Him, He will build His church. We don't need more people in church; we need close communion with Him. We don't need numbers; we need the ability to hear Him, and we need His power to respond properly to His instructions. The *perceived* need for numbers will drive congregations toward compromise and popularity. Recognizing the *real* need for communion and obedience will drive people to seek His face in all of life. It will drive us to obedience without regard to consequence, and obedience will cause the powers and principalities in the heavenly realms to stand in awe of God.

Perceptions of purpose determine plans and actions. We don't depend upon numbers; we depend upon Christ!

Following right designs allows for success. Notice that I did not say that right design "guarantees" success. There is always the possibility someone might use a "hammer" for a "screwdriver." However, misuse of that well designed hammer not only causes the chaos of stripping the screw, but it insults the designer of the hammer and the screw. It is obvious that even well designed devices in the hands of ignorant users will cause problems. The perfectly designed hammer and the reputation of its designer are only "safe" in the hands of a person who knows the correct purpose and design for the thing before he picks up the instrument. Success comes only when the designer's purpose, the right tool, and sufficient power are married together beautifully in truth. Only then can the house be properly built. However, proper design is only a beginning. The real trick is to achieve and maintain intimate communion with the designer. He is the only one who knows the real purpose, capabilities, and limitations of the design and the product.

Bad results betray poor design and/or following wrong ideas. This may be obvious, but I often wonder why it is that, in our struggle to solve the problems in our lives and society, we continue to turn to the flawed institutions of Church and Government for help. We pay our dues to both, we take their advice, and we work hard to implement their suggestions; but the problems get larger and more complex. Then we run straight back to the Church and Government; we spend more time, more money, invest more personal resources and, in the end, we only reap more chaos. Our lives seem hopelessly lost in this downward spiral, but we keep going back to the same old institutions.

I am reminded of a story about Joseph Stalin. He was once asked why he tormented his own people so much. To illustrate his answer, he picked up a live chicken and proceeded to pluck out its feathers one by one. He did this plucking while he was talking about how to get people to follow him. At the end, he sat the chicken on the ground and walked off. The chicken followed him around like a pet puppy. He even tried to out run the chicken; but the creature stuck close to its tormentor in a sort of panicked, perverted dependency. Rather a graphic picture, don't you think?

I've noticed that it is not only chickens who seek the "safety" of evil entities. People are doing the same thing with the institutions I mentioned earlier. There are many in torment and bondage who prefer the familiarity of a devil they know to the unfamiliar peace and freedom in Christ. Someone is wrongheaded here, or something is wrong with the design; or, maybe, it is both!

Crossed-Purposes

If people depend upon a thing and you control that thing, then you control everyone who depends upon it. The government is keenly aware of this and uses it to its advantage. The institution of the church is keenly aware of it and is using it as well. And, what is really insidious is, the two institutions are becoming so co-mingled they are beginning to look like one and the same. If that sounds shocking or ludicrous to you, then you are in for a real education.

Most churches are registered with the IRS as "501(C)(3) Non-Profit Corporations." This enables the members of the church to deduct their contributions or "tithe" from their income taxes. In order to keep this nonprofit status, a church has to follow IRS guidelines. This has become a cattle prod in the hands of our anti-Christian government, enabling it to push church leadership into line at the slaughterhouse of 'politically correct' teaching.

It goes like this: "If we don't conform to the model set up by government, we can lose our tax exempt status. If we lose that, we lose membership and money. If we lose membership and money, we lose our jobs. Better to compromise 'just a little' with the Devil than to lose our jobs. We can't talk about *political candidates* here; oh, no! That would really do us in. No, we mustn't do that! They don't mind if we talk about sin in this building as long as certain sins aren't mentioned. Mentioning some of them would be considered a *hate crime*... can't do that either. The *EEOC* isn't all bad. They help the disadvantaged you know. Homosexuals need work too, don't they? And besides, if we go ahead and hire them in our churches like the government says, maybe we can lead them to the Lord. No, we can't talk about the *second amendment* here. It's about self-defense and *guns*, and they might think we encourage those *constitutional militias.* That would surely cost us all. We'd better just stick to the standard sermonettes that tickle the ears every Sunday and leave the rest to the politicians. Besides, God doesn't really have anything to do with government, does He?"

Well, it should be pretty obvious at this point just how much the government controls speech when they control the pocket book. It should also be obvious the government actually gives the church permission to exist! The frightening thing is that the government, at this point in history, is at crossed-purposes with God's design for the church. The government's purpose and goal is to secularize the church - to change it into a *politically correct* entity. The government has abandoned its God-intended purpose and has become a "god" in its own eyes. Like all gods, this secular god is jealous and will not stand for competition. Everything is upside down now. At the genesis of our nation, men of God gave government permission to exist. But now government has taken the role of creator to the church and grants her permission to exist!

While the government is busy being god to the church, the church has been retreating to a reductionist Christianity. By that I mean the church has become consumed with numbers. The more that get "saved," the more the money pours into the coffers. The more money we have, the better we can be at "winning souls for the Lord." More souls, in turn, will equal more money. More money will enable them to build bigger institutions.

Leading people to Christ as their Savior is a noble and high calling, but it is the beginning of a process God has in mind for the believer. The church has forgotten the process! The church has forgotten *discipling.* Once a person is born again and receives his learner's permit, the real struggle begins. "How should we then live?" is a question put forth by Francis Schaeffer in a book entitled the same and is the most important question of all next to salvation. The tragedy is, the Body of Christ is in a total state of confusion over this question. We either give completely wrong answers, or we are

41

lead to depend upon wrong people for whatever right answers we can glean from a system that has forgotten its purpose.

I want to tell you of a real life adventure. There is a man I'll call Joshua, who was a deacon in the largest "church" in his community. He was a Bible teacher and counselor and was respected and trusted within the "organization." Something happened about three years ago that changed this man's thinking in reference to the "organized" church. It started several years after President Clinton's influence had caused a large number of Christians, including Joshua, to become extremely concerned about the state of our nation. In his discussions with people about the "state of the union," Joshua began to notice a few of his brothers were getting involved with constitutional militias. *(Now this is not a discussion about the Biblical and Constitutional validity of militias. That's for another writing. This is about the 501(C)(3) Corporate Church, so don't get side tracked here.)* He sought these friends out and asked them what led them in that direction.

As they talked, Joshua began to see a pattern. The "church" wasn't addressing the issues that were important to these men. It *couldn't* address them without offending the IRS! So these brothers simply drifted off and began to assemble together to discuss those issues among themselves with little or no Biblical influence. As time went by and Biblical influence became close to nil, the rhetoric these men utilized to express their discontent with the state of things became more inflammatory; danger wasn't far off. Joshua could see this dangerous trend and started discussing it with one of his dearest and closest brothers. Together they concluded it would be a good idea to invite these militia guys to a Bible study. Sounds like a great idea, but they were struck full in the face with a huge problem before they got off the ground. Where would they hold such a class?

Joshua didn't want to expose his "church" to the wrath of the government (that 501(C)(3) trap!) Since the "church" campus was out as an option, he decided to have it at the store where he worked. On the first night, seventy-two people came to hear what the Bible says about guns and governments. God was lifted up to those people' and in a matter of weeks, their hearts began to soften.

They began to change their attitudes and the extremism began to fade. But, in that same time frame, this Bible study caught the attention of the "leadership" of his church. Joshua was called into the office of the Executive Elder. Sounds a lot like being called to the principal's office, doesn't it? Well, it was a lot like it! Only the impact was far more weighty in Joshua's life. He was told he was not to associate with "those people." He was told that he was putting the "church" in danger and that "there is no place in America for Christians and guns!" Joshua was amazed at such a remark and responded by saying, "What about Washington, Jefferson, Adams and the rest of the founders? They thought it was a God-given right to keep and bear arms so the citizens could protect themselves from any malevolent government that might eventually come to power on this soil!" The elder responded, "That was then; this is now! And, we just won't have one of our 'leaders' associating with that militia crowd!" Joshua, still amazed at such an attitude, posed the next obvious question to the man as he said, "Who then is going to minister to those guys? Who is going to see that they understand what God says about authorized and unauthorized killing?" The elder was not really impacted with the weight of those questions and simply said, "Well, I don't know; but it is not going to be anyone from this church!"

The point of tension was clear to Joshua. The "church" was now at crossed-purposes with the Gospel. It was more than apparent the mission of that "church" was to save itself, rather than try to save the brothers from the bondage of the hatred and discontent they had with the status quo. Jesus told us that we would know them *(believers)* by the way they *"love one another,"* and Joshua had just seen exactly the opposite of *love* in that man's response. What was he to do? To Joshua, the choice was clear. He responded by offering an immediate solution to the elder's "problem." He resigned from the Board of Deacons right there on the spot.

Tragedies like this are all too familiar to those of us who have been in the church for any length of time. This "Elder" has completely missed the purpose for the Church. He has redesigned Her in his own mind. It is understandable that he would try to protect his institution because he sees all the "good" it does in the community. However, like so many others out there, he has misunderstood something critical about purpose. Specifically, he has misunderstood the purpose of the Church.

Both Joshua and Amy have fallen victim to men with wrong ideas about the way God intends for things to work. Their lives have been frustrated because what were supposed to be firm foundations for life, turned out to be institutional quicksand. Let's excavate a little farther and see if we can find some bed rock of truth upon which the foundation can be rebuilt.

Chapter 3

Foundations or Frustrations

Steve Donaldson

The Problem

I believe the problem we face today within the Bride of Christ, among our families and as individuals stems from our lack of understanding about the purpose for things. Unless one understands the purpose for a thing, he will abuse it. This abuse can take many forms, but for our discussion, abuse is defined as: *abnormal use of something - using it in any way outside it's creator's purpose.*

Since we live in a universe created by and for God, it would be a good idea to know why He made it. What was His purpose? God, like all manufacturers, saw the end of the project before He started. His *purpose* is the reason He created "all things." He had something in His mind before He began; something He wanted to accomplish. Perhaps in learning His purpose, we can set about working *with* Him toward that purpose.

If we don't understand the ultimate purpose of the Church, the Bride of Christ, then we will abuse Her. This Bride was created to be free, rested, and available to Her Husband! The yoke of Her Husband is easy and light. He has invited Her into His Sabbath rest, and His intention is for Her to be available to Him alone for His purpose. Anything that makes Her unavailable to Him is abusive! We are given clues to His specific purpose for His Bride throughout Scripture, but the starting place must be the back of the book. An author always ends his book by revealing his final purpose. What do we find at the back of The Book? We find a glorious, purified Bride in union with Him in heaven. He saw Her in Heaven beside Her Bridegroom before He ever said, "Let there be light!"

Since His purpose was and is to create this Bride for His Son and be glorified in the process, all of history and all of reality must be viewed within that context, whether work, play, family, country, politics, peace, war, or any other thing. There is no "secular" area of life. Life must be seen through and lived according to His purpose. Anyone who views life and history outside the context of God's intention to "create and perfect the Bride" will find himself at cross-purposes with his Creator. Such opposition to His purpose will lead to a great deal of difficulty and frustration in a person's life; it will also result in a lot of misery for the people around him.

Well, we have defined the purpose – but how is it to be accomplished? Just how does He gain this Bride for His Son? This is the foundation stone, and if we miss it, a chaos will ensue that will cripple not only the Church, but society as a whole.

The Process: An Introduction

The Gospel of Jesus Christ is the method God has put in place to bring about His purpose of creating the Bride. And this Gospel, The Good News of Jesus Christ, is the most misunderstood, yet the most foundational concept in His creation. There is more deception about the Gospel than any other aspect of Scripture because the enemy's attacks are focused there, so I'm compelled to focus there also.

Don't be tempted to skip this part! You may think you know the truth of the Gospel, that you are a mature enough, and that this is elementary for you. However, might be surprised. The only person who has permission to skip this part is the one who knows God's purpose for him as an individual. You can skip this part if you are confident you have eternal life and if your life is free of problems in your relationships. To skip this section, you must also be free of worry and stress, and exhibit the fruit of the Spirit in all

46

areas of your life. If that's you, skip a few paragraphs. Otherwise you might want to stick around and see what lies ahead.

Before I go farther, I want to remind you that all of life for you and your family depends upon how well you grasp this concept. Your comprehension of the truth exposed here will determine how well you fare in future crisis. It will impact your motives for all of life. And if you think this is unimportant, you must be educated to the fact that *motives determine choices*. All the decisions you make in life, whether business, personal, financial, or any other kind, depend upon your motive for doing things. Doing right things for wrong reasons has been the cause for many a failure. Make no mistake here. Get this down into your very soul. Understanding this concept will make all the difference in the world in how you fare in the days ahead.

At this time I ask the Lord Jesus to enable your spirit to hear His Holy Spirit and to give you discernment for truth. Spiritual truth isn't learned; it is revealed. It is revealed from His Word into your spirit. I am going to ask you to read His Word and pray about what you read. The Spirit will reveal His truth to you as you read His Word, but only if you're not too spiritually noisy to hear. So be quiet! Don't take my word for this. Don't follow tradition or what others have told you about the truth. Take Him at His Word, and the truth will become evident to you. You will be able to understand how He plans to accomplish His purpose and how the whole process works through the Gospel, the Good News of Christ crucified and raised from the dead. It is your choice, your responsibility, your life, and your future. His Word never returns void, so I implore you to read His Word!

The Plight of Man

Since the fall of Adam in the Garden of Eden, everyone has been born with two problems which separate them from God. *First*, all men are born spiritually dead. To be dead means one is no longer *available* for communion with others. For example, a dead human body is no longer available to the person who once lived there. The wages of sin is death: *spiritual death*. That first sin killed all of mankind spiritually. It left all of us eternally separated from God because God is Spirit, and a spiritually dead man is no longer able to commune with Him. When Adam sinned, he and all his offspring were removed from communion with Him. *Secondly*, we are all born sinners. We are not sinners because we sin; we sin because we are born sinners! We inherited the plight in our kinship with Adam.

This is man's plight. We are dead to God because of Adam. Even if we were made *spiritually* alive to Him, we would experience a very short life because of our personal sin. The wages of sin is death. Even if it were possible to live a totally sinless life, we would still be eternally separated from God because we are dead to Him through our earthly father Adam. Since one must be both spiritually alive and completely free from sin in order to enter into His presence in Heaven there is an inescapable horror before us: we are all dead sinners with no hope of avoiding eternal damnation! Where is the answer to man's plight?

The answer lies in the love of God for His creation. Because He loves us, He began the answer to our plight by showing us the hopelessness of our condition before Him. God gave us the Law to serve as a mirror that will show us all how guilty we are in His presence. He gave it to us to show us we have no hope of attaining a perfect sin-free life and are locked out of 'life' and union with Him in heaven. And through this Law, we are driven to a different solution, one that can overcome the fact that we are all dead in sin and no one can live a sin-free life. Through His love for us, God has offered a twofold solution to man's twofold problem.

The Love of God

Since we are sinners in our core, God giving us life would be a futile act because we would only sin again. God had to provide a way to take care of the sin problem – *all* of the sin problem. Someone must pay for the offence of sin, someone must die! And by making this provision in advance for all the sin of all the people, He can give life to the dead and assure at the same time there is no way for it to be lost again! That is His purpose. Before the foundation of the world, the Cross of Christ was in the mind of God to be the vehicle where the Lamb would be slain and, thereby, be the provision for *all* the sins of the people. The Cross of Christ is the solution for the *second plight* of man, which is that we are all born sinners.

This is an important point. God operates *outside* our space-time continuum, totally outside of time. Christ was on the cross from the beginning of the world paying continually for all sins of all men! He died to pay for all sin for all time, and all that is left for the people is to accept the provision!

Now, since sin has been paid for, God can go about the task of giving His life, eternal life, to those who believe in Him. He was delivered to death on the cross because of our offenses and was raised from the dead to secure our justification. Now He will grant life eternal, a life that cannot be taken away and a life that never ends, to all who will believe in Him and what He has done! He will never charge any of our sins to our account again, and we cannot die spiritually, ever! We will live for and with Him forever! The resurrection of Christ is the solution for the *first plight* of man, which is that we were all born dead to God.

Jesus is *the solution* to both of our problems. He paid for all our sins, and He will give His eternal life to anyone who believes!

Now, that's Good News! Now, my motives can change! Now, I can get back into the fight. Now, I can walk without fear within His purpose for me, with praise on my lips, and with thanksgiving in my heart!

This is the foundation stone. The Cross of Christ and His resurrection alone, without any self-righteousness and without any work at all on my part, are sufficient to bring me to life and keep me there. To speak otherwise is to *trample the cross of Christ under foot and to count it of no effect!* (Hebrews 10:29) As believers we are alive and free in Christ to become all that He created us to be! Now, we can function properly within this Body, this Bride of His!

49

Availability

The Bible teaches that God loved me while I was still a dead sinner and that He will love me without condition – always! Good or bad performance isn't an issue with His love. Only when you see that, can you understand what Paul told Titus when he said we do good works because they are good and profitable to people. Work isn't good because of what it is, it is good only by its origin. If it is from Him through you for the good of others, you will never experience stress, fatigue, or burnout. It won't even feel like work. If it is from you because you or someone else "thought" that's what you're supposed to do to please God, then you are going to find that the wheels fall off of your life in many areas. Servanthood which is properly motivated, e.g. motivated by the Holy Spirit, will never cost a family their Prophet, Priest, or King. It will never cheat the family of the companionship, nurture, care and proper teaching of the wife and mother.

God has a purpose for you; and if you go off on your own, or someone else's *purposeful* agenda, you will miss His plan for your life. You and those around you will suffer the consequences of doing right things for wrong reasons.

Jesus wants you free to become all that He created you to become! If you are off doing someone else's agenda, you are becoming what you or *they* want you to become instead. You have only one Master, and His name is Jesus. You and your family can't afford to listen to anyone but Him about what, where, and when you are to do things. If you wind up following some rigid agenda for "spiritual growth" provided to you by some organization, you won't be available to Christ and His purpose for you. You will be busy following their agenda. Church leaders who are genuinely interested in true discipling are going to try to help you toward that goal of being all you can be *in Christ*. This Bride was created to be available to Christ! She is to be available to Him and no one else. As an individual, you are to be His – not yours!

But over the years, religious organizations have adopted a process to try to get people to follow an agenda instead of trying to teach them how to be available to Christ. They have started programs and instituted numbers games. And they have implemented some common tactics to get the numbers up for all the programs. The tactic? Make them feel guilty. How can a Bride be Herself and give Herself completely when someone sets about to make her operate out of guilt?

I was once asked to give a talk to the parents of teenagers in our church in order to encourage them to come to a weekly prayer meeting that would meet at 6 am. An assistant pastor whispered in my ear and said, "If you lay a good guilt trip on them, more will come!" If I've ever been tempted to do bodily harm to a preacher, it was then! Guilt is a great motivator, isn't it? You were not designed by God to handle guilt. Keeping guilt will make you both spiritually and physically.

Guilt must go somewhere. The Cross of Christ is where guilt was taken away. If you don't give it to Him, you will be very easy to manipulate. It's a carrot on a stick. You can never reach it. You will never be able to give enough, change enough, or do enough in all the programs they have lined up for you. I can tell you this for certain, if the church you go to now uses guilt to motivate you, you need to get out of there! It is not Jesus doing that to you. He motivates with love and compassion. He gives you the desires of your heart. He creates a desire in your heart to give and to do with grace, thanksgiving, and joy. The choice is yours. You may either give your guilt to Him or be manipulated into uselessness.

The Bride is Meant to be Attractive

The Body was created to be – and will become – an attractive Bride. But how many times have you heard anyone say, "Oh! I'd just love to be a Christian!?" We generally have quite the opposite effect upon those around us. On a more personal level, how many times have you had someone say, "I'd love to be just like you!"

Our Lord told us of only two ways to judge whether a person has Life in Him. He said we can know them *by the way they love their brothers in the Lord and by their fruit*. The question then becomes, what is this fruit? Some would say it's the work done in the name of the Lord, or the righteousness manifest in the person's

51

life or the number of people a person has "led to the Lord." No, the fruit of the "Spirit" can *lead* to those, but it is *not* those things. The fruit of the Spirit is love, joy, peace, patience, goodness, kindness, meekness, faithfulness, and self-control. These are simply the character traits of Christ Himself. All but one are a set of attitudes about life and what goes on in it. Notice that the scripture does not say these are the "fruits" of the Spirit. It is "fruit" singular – *one fruit*, different segments of the *same* orange. At the beginning, these segments are all immature. They grow as a person's view of God becomes clear and His faithfulness becomes more apparent to the believer. If a person believes he isn't safe with Christ because he has been wrongly taught that God will throw him away for not being "confessed up" or for committing one too many sins or for sinning "on purpose," then the fruit will stop growing and may waste away. It cannot mature in that environment.

If you find yourself in a such a place – one which teaches a *no good news* gospel, then you really need to get out of there. If you stay, you will observe a lot of really mean spirited, condemning, self-righteous, manipulative "do-gooders" who are devoid of the attitudes of Christ. So, for the sake of your communion with Christ and the safety of your family and friends, get out now! The Lord loves them too, and He will deal with them in His own way, but now you know better, so remove yourself and place yourself under His wing alone. You don't have time to sit and argue theology. Once you have left that environment, He will begin to heal immediately and the fruit will begin to mature and your life will be filled with joy!

Agapé and its Requirements

Notice, I said earlier all but *one* of the segments of the fruit is an attitude. The one segment of the fruit that is not an attitude, requires commitment, and has nothing whatsoever to do with feelings or attitudes: it is *love*. In the Greek, the word *love* has four renditions in English. The one which applies to our discussion is called *agapé*. It is a love which only God can express in its purest form and which we can only express as He enables us. This *agapé* love of God is a commitment. It is not an emotion. The importance of this type love is demonstrated by the description Christ gave to its weightiness when He said, "The entire Law and all of the works of the Prophets hang upon this word (*agapé*)."

The significance of this concept of love being a commitment becomes clear when you place it in the context of Christ's commandment to us to *love* our enemies. Few people realize the word for love in this context is *agapé*. So what does the commandment "love your enemies," really mean? There have been volumes written, studies done, lectures heard, and lives spent trying to understand this *love* of God. If you take all those volumes, lectures, and studies and distill them into one crystalline drop, *agapé* is defined as the commitment to serve the best interest of the beloved regardless of the cost. *Agapé* translates into a commitment on my part to serve your best interest no matter what it costs me or what it costs you!

Sounds simple, doesn't it? But it requires that you know what is in someone's best interest. And no human can know what the best interest of another human will be in every circumstance. Only God can know what is in anyone's best interest. By definition we have just locked out the unbelievers, or the "dead ones," from being capable of truly loving anyone. They are *dead* men and have no communion with God: they cannot know His mind so they cannot know the best interests of anyone. Only a "Living," Spirit-filled person has the capacity to know God's mind through communion with Him and is, therefore, able to know the best interests of others. We have the mind of Christ, so we can know. It is not something we have to "figure out." It may or may not appear to be the "logical" thing, but this knowledge is going to be both Biblical and intuitive. You will just know. And that knowledge will always line up with His Word.

Another requirement of *agapé* is motive. It is a "no matter the cost" issue. God alone is selfless enough to act on behalf of our best interests by giving His all on the cross. No matter what it costs *HIM,* He serves our best interests; and no matter how much it costs *US,* He does the same. Since believers have the mind of Christ, we have the God given ability to respond in like manner to others. But if I am committed to serving the best interests of others, I become vulnerable as I go about loving them selflessly. So who is going to watch my back while I am trying to make you the first, and the most, and the winner? Who is going to take care of me while I serve you? It is Jesus. He will send someone or something for me if I need it, but where does that motive come from? That is a love that comes from God alone, it is not in man to do things like that. And since a lost person ultimately does everything for "self," even the seemingly "good" and benevolent things are done with selfish motives. Therefore, a lost man cannot have *agapé* motives for anything.

The last requirement of *agapé* is the "power" to accomplish the best interests of others. C.S. Lewis said, "love (*agapé*) demands the perfecting of the beloved" and one must have the power to perform that action. The power required to perform that action is "faith" – not faith in faith, but faith in God Himself. It is His power at work here after all, not ours. It is error to think that we can get more faith as we go. The fact is we have all we need; it is a matter of learning what can be done with what we have. The ability to exercise our faith grows as we learn more about God. And we learn the character of God through experience and revelation. As He turns up the dimmer switch and enlightens His character and reveals more of Himself along the way we are able to exercise our faith more fully and more completely.

So you see, it is all dependent upon Him; it is His *agapé*, His motive, His knowledge, His power. The commitment on our part is to trust Him to *agapé* us and supply all our needs.

Recipients of agape are always made better. If you want things to get better, trust the Lord, not men. Understand His purpose, and bring your life into line with that purpose. Understand the design. Only the manufacturer knows the complete set of capabilities and limitations of His product. He will never take you to a place of danger: but men will and, traditions will. If your life seems stressful or lacks purpose and meaning, if you are not fulfilled, then you're going to the wrong physician. Stop taking the recipes for success offered by men and their man-made institutions. Come to the Creator, the Great Healer.

Divine Deliverers.... or Dolphins

I don't want to leave this subject and give you the impression I believe the "institutional church" is full of bad people being led by bad people. I believe it is generally filled with believers who are sincere and who have proper motives. I am just trying to point out the "church" is the only game in town, and its participants have been held to mediocrity by a system which has been flawed for over 1700 years! Many times the leaders are looked up to as "divine deliverers" of the *lost* or *misguided* in their "flock." They are looked upon as what might be called "spiritual" and "emotional" lifeguards. Granted they rescue some, but their efforts remind me more of dolphins than lifeguards. You might have heard dolphins have pushed many potential drowning victims to shore, thereby saving a life. Well, it turns out, dolphins just like to push things, and they push just as many things out to sea as they do onto the shore! They might *drown* a swimmer as often as they *save* one.

Although the results they produce might be poor and inconsistent, I frankly don't know many preachers, deacons, or elders who intentionally set out to harm the people in their churches. On the contrary, they really do see themselves as servants of the people. Many of them honestly believe the "institution" is the right tool to use to get the job done. These guys have a genuine affection for people; so they set up all kinds of programs, educational opportunities, and techniques for the people to follow to achieve "self-improvement." The problem is, as the people are encouraged to participate in the "programs and techniques," they become dependent upon them. Too many fail to develop an intimate and personal relationship with God.

Let me develop that point by letting you overhear something a pastor or deacon might be heard saying to a brand new member of the "church"...

"Listen, now that you're one of 'us" I know you'll want to get involved. You know, become part of the Jesus team. We all help each other to be really good, try really hard, and impact the world for Jesus. And by the way, we need some greeters for the front door. You can go see Bob over there just past the back desk where the offering plates are. Be sure to drop something in on your way by. You know, we all must give till it hurts – it is seed money for the 'church.' Grow, grow, grow.... takes seed and water, you know.

You say you've got problems in your family? Well, you might have sin in your life! I know we all have a few bad habits, but don't worry about anything, we have a program for any problem. We can all talk about that at the 6 a.m. men's breakfast on Tuesday. You'll want to be there for sure. The teacher is already covering *Step Seven*, but I'll help you learn the six you've missed. I gotta go now, see ya at the Monday night prayer group. All the really faithful come to that; it only lasts till about 9! You can leave your wife and kids with some of the special teachers trained just for their age group or hobby preferences. No, I don't know what they're teaching; but it must be good, people are really bonding with those teachers."

This guy really means well, doesn't he?. He's trying with all his might to help this new member. He has compassion and wants to please God with his good works; but he's pushing the new member toward programs and methods, instead of leading him in the direction God would have him go... into a peaceful, intimate, and personal relationship with His Father.

Since the "church" has misdirected the people to the programs and games instead of pointing them to an intimate, personal relationships with the Father, a false need has arisen within the church. Because the design is wrong, problems of living for the believer have become more frequent and severe. What is the solution the "organized church" came up with? Why... they developed a new breed of dolphin. He is called the *Christian counselor*. This "counselor" is another surrogate. He has taken the role from the rightful "priest" of the family. This surrogate priest has effectively robbed the man of the blessing of being the one trusted by his family to lead them through Christ to solutions for their problems. Notice how the role has changed hands over time in the church. God intended the man of the family to be their corporate priest; the *institutionalized church* stole the role and gave it to the pastor; and after many years they had to create a whole new subset of pastors called *counselors* in order to cope with all the chaos. Wouldn't it be best for the right corporate priest to simply step up, do his homework, and take his priesthood back?

American Christians have been led to believe that unless one has a degree or some special training, he isn't qualified as a problem solver. However, the Word says *He has given us all we need for life and godliness* (II Peter 1:3).

I know many sincere and caring people who are Christian counselors. They laugh with the people and cry with the people. They are personable, well loved, and respected for their ability to give people techniques to help the pain go away. But, making the pain go away is frequently the *wrong* thing to do. Sounds crazy, doesn't it? I hate to drop that idea and leave you hanging, but we will have to develop that idea later. Suffice it to say here - if someone is taught to depend upon any technique or person, other than Jesus Christ and His Word, for answers to the problems of living, he has been deceived. Any "real" advisor knows there is only one Counselor, and His name is Jesus. He is the One upon Whom we are to depend; after all, He is the Manufacturer, and only the Manufacturer knows all the problems his product might develop. Only the Manufacturer knows the proper fixes for His product.

A well informed preacher or teacher who understands it is not his role to be divine deliverer, wants to work himself out of a job as rapidly as possible. Teaching his "flock" to commune with the Father and gain an understanding of His character will enable those new believers to escape the prison of dependency upon men. It will enable them to step forward boldly into the freedom of dependency upon God alone! *The Lord is Spirit, and where the Spirit of the Lord is, there is liberty!* (II Corinthians 3:17)

I know the "institution" has helped lead many people to recognize their need of Christ as their Savior. It has also helped many of them achieve a certain level of maturity. But too often, the "institution" is like the dolphin. Anyone who's been a Christian for awhile knows some victims of spiritual dolphins. These are people who have been pushed off the course of productive Christianity and onto a course which leads them toward a sea of hurt, confusion, and doubt. These people are functionally out of the fight and tend to lead others around them right to the chaos. The good news here is, its precisely that reproof of chaos that God has used to awaken some of His sheep to the fact that something is wrong with a system that produces such chaos. In fact, it is this loving reproof that inspired this writing.

Dolphins are lovable and try really hard at being good dolphins, but if you don't want one to push you out to sea, you might be better off just to swim away. It is my hope and prayer that the Spirit of God will enlighten both the dolphin and all those swimmers out there to the truth that will cause them to be reborn into real men – men with God's view of life, men who will be tools He can use to redress the Body as His Bride, men He can use to get Her ready to meet Her Bridegroom, for the day of the wedding approaches.

I think there is hope for major change to take place within the Body of Christ. I believe we can get back on the right course. I believe she will be dressed beautifully when She meets her Bridegroom. But I believe any change which takes place must be based on the way God intended things to work, based on His original design, based on the goal of fulfilling His intended purpose for His creation. God started things out with institutions, and I believe in reinstating the institution of family which He intended to be the perfect model. The family is the only answer to the current ills befalling His Body.... His Bride. We have to use the institution of family the way God intended for us to use it. We have to get back to the original design, which is the building block for it all.

What about Amy?

If you are wondering what happened to the young lady at the beginning of this chapter, I told her to go home and ask her husband to become Prophet, Priest, and King of his home. I told her to ask Him to help her understand the role for a Bride in the Bible and to ask Him to teach her how Christ loves the church. They have real problems, and they are going to get a lot worse in a big hurry if they continue to rely upon the "hired ones" in the "institution" of the church or the government as their source of safety. For our well being, it is time to rely upon the Master and our Brothers and Sisters, someone without an axe to grind and not looking for personal gain and someone who can really *agapé*. Institutions can't *agapé*; only God and your Brothers and Sisters can do that.

We must *agapé* now! Time is too short, we must learn to survive as a Body in rapid fashion.

One of the best examples I've seen about teaching survival in crisis is the movie "The Earthling." The lesson can apply to almost any one for physical survival, or any group to ensure survival of relationships. If you need a lesson on how to survive in just a short period of time, this movie is a good one teacher.

The setting for "The Earthling" is the Australian wilderness, hundreds of miles from civilization. William Holden's character has a terminal disease and has gone out there on foot to a boyhood hideout to die in peace. Ricky Schroeder's character is about 8 years old, and his parents have just been killed in a horrible accident, leaving him abandoned and far from any help in the wilderness. Upon finding the boy, the man faces an awful set of circumstances. He is too ill to take the boy back to civilization; he'd die long before they reached help. If he helps the boy with food, water, and shelter, the boy will last only as long as the man remains alive. The dilemma is heart rending, but choices have to be made.

The man decides that the only chance the boy has for survival is to be taught quickly to fend for himself. The man knows the boy must be given the ultimate motivation to learn. William Holden's character sadly won't let the boy come near him. He lets him come just close enough so that he can see what the man is doing to survive. The man catches fish but won't let the boy have any fish to eat. The man makes fire with sticks but lets the boy shiver in the cold of the night. The man builds a shelter against the rain but won't let the boy come in and be dry. After several days of the boy watching what the man does to survive, he learns how to make a wooden spear and catch fish. He learns how to make a fire using just sticks. He watches the man make a shelter and makes one for himself. At the end, before the man dies, the boy has learned all the ways of survival and knows that he will be able to make it back to civilization alone. Only then does his hatred for the man turn to loving admiration. The boy has seen love in action, a love that truly serves the best interests of the beloved. Tough? Yes! But absolutely vital to the boy's survival.

I asked Amy to become like William Holden's character. I asked her to show her husband that he must learn what God says about family relationships or there would be an end to those relationships since the survival of his family depends upon him. Amy is eager to trust her husband with his role as Prophet, Priest, and King. She will not seek a surrogate for him again because she knows, if she does, she's actually cheating him and her entire family. They will need each other in their proper roles as we proceed through these last days, and the time to learn is now.

It is time to *loose the bands of wickedness, to undo the heavy burdens, and to let the oppressed go free, and that ye break every yoke?... to deal thy bread to the hungry, and that thou bring the poor that are cast out to thy house? when thou seest the naked, that thou cover him; and that thou hide not thyself from thine own flesh? Then shall thy light break forth as the morning, and thine health shall spring forth speedily: and thy righteousness shall go before thee; the glory of the LORD shall be thy rereward. Then shalt thou call, and the LORD shall answer; thou shalt cry, and he shall say, Here I am. If thou take away from the midst of thee the yoke, the putting forth of the finger, and speaking vanity; And if thou draw out thy soul to the hungry, and satisfy the afflicted soul; then shall thy light rise in obscurity, and thy darkness be as the noon day: And the LORD shall guide thee continually, and satisfy thy soul in drought, and make fat thy bones: and thou shalt be like a watered garden, and like a spring of water, whose waters fail not. And they that shall be of thee shall build the old waste places: thou shalt raise up the foundations of many generations; and thou shalt be called, The repairer of the breach, The restorer of paths to dwell in... Then shalt thou delight thyself in the LORD; and I will cause thee to ride upon the high places of the earth, and feed thee with the heritage of*

Jacob thy father: for the mouth of the LORD hath spoken it....
(Isaiah 58:6-12, 14)

Sometimes progress is actually a turning around, and this is one of those times. When we realize that we've taken the wrong road, the only sensible thing to do is to return to the last fork and correct our direction. We must return to the foundation set up by God. The *families* not the *man-made institutions* are the building blocks for His Bride.

The Lord has told us that *all who desire to live godly in Christ Jesus will suffer persecution.* (II Timothy 3:12) We must return to His model. The model we currently use is a NOT model for persecution, but ultimate destruction. We've not been set up for persecution. We've been set up to be so ineffective, confused, compromising and generally pathetic that any potential persecutors might just walk right past us without noticing at all. The official "church" in Russia and in China suffer no persecution, and we are rapidly becoming like them! In our current state, we are no real threat to the world system, and that is the saddest indictment of all. If we remain the same, we will become scattered, and helpless. Our children will have no godly heritage to remember and pass on. The New World Order will take us without a fight, and the Church as an institution in America will die! If you look back at history, you will find nothing to encourage you to reach any other conclusion. No country that has gained a Christian center and then let it slip away has ever recovered Christ-centeredness. They have all just slipped away into nothingness.

I don't know if we have time – only the Lord knows that! – but we must begin now! We are directed to provide for our families or be seen as worse than infidels. That provision begins and ends with Jesus Himself. Because He gives us the correct model for His Bride, our job, even our duty as Christians, is to become all that He created us to be. He wants a Bride who is available to the Him, making choices with *agapé.*

Chapter 4

Moral Choices
Steve Donaldson

The Adventure Begins

It is apparent the institutions of Church, Family, and Government in our society are quite ill. It is also apparent that we are heading for chaos as a result of that illness. We are faced with kids killing kids, wars, a hollow economic system, and political unrest both here and abroad. In the light of these conditions, we have some difficult choices in store for us. Before we reach the intersections where choices must be made, we must be sure we are properly prepared to make these decisions. Making godly decisions with *agapé* will fulfill the Creator's purpose and will yield a bounty of Spiritual fruit.

Like everyone else, I want my family to be safe and secure. I have children and grandchildren, and I'm dedicated to looking after their well-being. Jacob is 6, Hannah is 5, Kaleb is 3, and Joseph is 2. These children are a wonder to me. Their lives are a continual adventure, full of mystery, awe and excitement. The only time they have a problem is when someone interrupts the adventure with the mundane, the seemingly unnecessary, or the uncomfortable. Things like baths, naps, broccoli, and doctors' offices are not welcome because they delay the adventure.

There is very little worry in a child's life because he has someone he trusts who watches over him. Children are usually not conscious of it, but deep down they know they are safe in the hands of someone who loves them and has the ability to care properly for them.

Our Lord intends for our lives to be just like that of children! We know more than a child does about the realities of life, but the perspective should be the same. The adventure should begin now and should last for the rest of our lives.

The Lord wants us to have a life of rest and peace. *Come unto me, all ye that labour and are heavy laden, and I will give you rest. Take my yoke upon you, and learn of me; for I am meek and lowly in heart: and ye shall find rest unto your souls. For my yoke is easy, and my burden is light* (Matthew 11:28-30).

But how we can have a life of rest, peace, and real adventure, when societal collapse appears just around the corner? How can we relax and be full of joy when we have no idea what our world is going to be like in the future?

Uncertainty and Fear

When most people, realize the magnitude of the problems around us, they become anxious. Anxiety is the first visceral response to crisis. The questions come in like a confusing flood. There are so many decisions to make right now, and with limited knowledge and resources, frustration comes easily. I don't know any Christian who doesn't want to be obedient to the will of God. The problem is knowing His will. And in order to know His will one must be a good listener. Even in good times, most have trouble hearing Him. However, during crisis people usually scream so loud they can't hear His voice at all. If they can't hear His voice, they cannot possibly obey His commands. The frustrations and anxiety of crisis can be deafening and cause even believers to err in our choices.

What do I do? For what conditions do I prepare? What am I supposed to have? Where am I supposed to go? What about my extended family and friends? How many can I accommodate? How should I approach others with a warning? Am I to prepare or just trust God or both? Where am I going to get the necessary resources for all of this?

These questions become more complex as the details of preparedness begin to come into focus. All of this can be a very bewildering experience. There are answers to these questions, but the most important question of all has yet to be asked. The primary question should be, *"Why am I asking?"* The reason this should be the first question on your list is because *motives determine choices!*

I'll leave it in other capable hands to discuss the details of all the former questions while I focus upon the last. *What are your motives?*

Why do you want to be ready for coming events? If *security* is your motive, then how far are you willing to go to protect you and yours? Are you willing to kill another person to preserve "your stuff?"

If *survival is* your motive, then what price are you willing to pay to survive? Are you willing to make the hard choices that may have life long consequences? For instance, suppose a family with children comes to you for food and shelter. Will you provide for them knowing every bite of food you give them is a bite your children won't have? Will you turn them away to starve and freeze in order to save food and fuel for your own children? What if you have to shoot the dad in front of his children to keep him from stealing food from the mouths of your children? There may be decisions to make just like that in the near future. So what is your motive?

Are you preparing from a sense of duty to your family and community or from a desire to minister to others and exercise biblical stewardship?

There are myriads of other possible motives ranging from profit to evangelism. Most people are motivated by some combination of motives mixed with a little fear and apprehension. Generally, at least at the beginning, motives are a little unclear. Although usually they are the last things on the minds of people, motives are the first and most important things from God's perspective. He says, *The spirit of man is the candle of the LORD, searching all the inward parts of the belly.* (Proverbs 20:27) To

God, the "why" is more important than the "what" of a situation. Proper motives will not always guarantee proper actions, but *improper motives* always betray a deceived or ignorant heart. Deceived or ignorant men are never trustworthy, so God says, *There is a way which seemeth right unto a man, but the end thereof are the ways of death.* (Proverbs 14:12)

The Purpose for the Adventure

Before we can properly explore our motives, we must know the *standard motive*. The *standard motive* is the motive by which all motives must be measured to assure correctness. The standard is always the Lord Himself. We must ask the question, "As viewed from God's perspective, why is all this happening?" If we can know why God is doing certain things, or allowing an event to happen, then we can confidently check *our* motives against *His* purpose. As I stated in the previous chapter, a *purpose* is the reason, or motive for one's actions. If our motive lines up with God's purpose, then we are working toward the same goal as God and will find things being blessed as we go. If, on the other hand, our motives are not in line with His purpose, then whatever we do will put us at *crossed-purposes* with the Creator of the universe. Since being at crossed-purposes with the Creator is an automatic default to failure, our actions cannot be blessed.

As I mentioned earlier, no manufacturer ever creates a product without first having the purpose for that product in his mind. So, the purpose for anything exists in the mind of the creator before he creates it. We must conclude God's purpose for the universe as a whole, and you individually, was conceived in His mind prior to Genesis 1:1. Once we find that grand and general purpose, we will be able to check our motives against His to see if they are in line with His plan.

The purpose for this whole adventure is to complete the Bride of Christ! In order to obtain that perfected Bride, all of human history has to function according to His purpose; and in the end, the Bride will be complete. *Here is your purpose*, because here is the grand and complete purpose of God in the universe.

Every person has a part to play in the perfection of the Bride, whether saved or lost, each has his role. The vast majority will never be conscious of their part, but we are different. We have a known purpose, a known mission. We may not know the details until the time comes, but just knowing God's purpose for us will have an enormous impact on the choices we make.

Before He created the earth, He determined *our time and the boundaries of our habitation* (Acts 17:26). We were created for the here and now. No other people in history were created for this time, so we are uniquely qualified for our purpose. But to what specific purpose are we called?

Repent and Obey

Since the goal is to conform our purpose to His, obedience is our first purpose. We must obey without hesitation or regard for consequence in order to be effective in our purpose. I have taught my family to respond to my direction without question in time of crisis, and God would have us respond to Him in the same way. We must *repent* from our ways and *obey* His.

The first step toward obedience is repentance. Repentance is the heart or state of mind that enables obedience. And it is the goodness of God that leads to repentance. When He reveals His purpose and His faithfulness, we see His goodness which changes the desires of our heart. Repentance is a gift from God, enabling the *desire* to obey; and faith gives us the power to obey.

The following references will enable you to quickly observe the method He uses to teach obedience:

James 1:2-4 – *My brethren, count it all joy when you fall into divers temptations; Knowing this, that the trying of your faith worketh patience. But let patience have her perfect work, that ye may be perfect and entire, wanting nothing.*

Romans 5:3 – *And not only so, but we glory in tribulations also: knowing that tribulation worketh patience; And patience, experience; and experience, hope: And hope maketh not ashamed; because the love of God is shed abroad in our hearts by the Holy Ghost which is given unto us.*

Hebrews 5:8 – *Though he were a Son, yet learned he obedience by the things which he suffered.*

Proverbs 29:19 – *A servant will not be corrected by words: for though he understand he will not answer.*

Psalms 119:67 – *Before I was afflicted I went astray, but now have I kept thy word.*

Psalms 119:71 – *It is good for me that I have been afflicted, that I might learn thy statutes.*

Psalms 119:75 – *I know, O LORD, that thy judgments are right, and that thou in faithfulness hast afflicted me.*

Psalms 119:92 – *Unless thy law had been my delight, I should then have perished in mine affliction.*

God has told us in Hebrews 5:8 that Christ *learned obedience by the things that He suffered*; and we will learn by the same method. He obviously doesn't see pain and suffering, trials and reproofs as we usually see them. God sees all uncomfortable situations as good for us. He works out all things together for good for those who love Him and are called according to His purpose. Obedience to God is our purpose, our fulfillment, our duty station if you will. But it seems the human, even the regenerate human, cannot obey without trials and reproofs thrown in as tests and discipline.

Sudden catastrophic changes, threats to our well being, temptations, or challenges to the status quo happen to all of us at one time or another. And it would not be uncommon to hear a Christian in crisis think, "What is going on here? Why is this happening to me? Why do the bad people seem to be getting along just fine and here I am trying to be all God wants me to be and I am suffering like the devil? After all, now that I am a Christian, shouldn't things be getting better?" These thoughts have occurred to every Christian who has gone through suffering and difficulty. And when these thoughts come, we must remember He has a purpose for all things, even difficult things. His primary concern is the perfecting of the Bride. Nothing else matters outside that context! In other words, life, liberty, property, family, etc., matter only as they are used to perfect the Bride!

Everything happens to perfect you! All of the life is working together for your good so you can become all that you were created to be! You were created to be the obedient Bride of Christ, to be one with Him! His life is in you. As a matter of fact, His life is the only real, eternal life in the universe. We died with Him on the cross so we have eternal life through Him here and now. We have exchanged our life for His. All of *life* will make sense only when we realize we died with Him and it is now only Him that lives! We are here so His life can be lived out here on earth and He can manifest Himself to people through us. His life is exhibited best in us through the difficulties of living. Anyone can look good in the good times! It is during the difficult times *Christ in us* has opportunity to shine. Only death to self can bring out the real life in us, Jesus Himself! Death to self makes proper response to adversity possible. The fruit of the Spirit grows to maturity as self-life dies! The Bride is perfected through obedience, and obedience is learned by suffering. Obedience fulfills our purpose and His!

Death to self is facilitated by discomfort; suffering motivates us to change and to seek the Lord. Temptation tests the change. Pain, suffering, and temptations shatter our old ideas and concepts of reality and make room for new growth! Death to self occurs as we are put into situations where we have no answers and no means of escape of our own. We can have the *peace that passeth all understanding* (Philippians 4:7) as we reckon ourselves dead and realize it is Christ in us, who is *our only hope of glory.* Our knowledge of His faithfulness, combined with our suffering enable us to obey Him. And as we obey Him, He will produce the fruit of the Spirit for us to bear unto maturity. The fruit of the Spirit as listed in Gal. 5:22-23 is simply *the character of Christ* developed within a person over time with testing. Our job is not to produce, but to simply rest patiently in Him through our testing until the fruit matures and hangs on us as an attractive bait for people, and a glory to God.

Pressure and Stress

Life during these times can make us so noisy we won't be able to Hear Him. If we cannot hear Him, we cannot obey Him. Unless we can silence the noise, we are functionally useless to our Lord. The noise of which I speak is brought about by the pressure upon us through various circumstances and conditions in our lives. We have all had pressure and felt emotional stress in our lives. Pressure and stress are going to be even more common in the future, so we must understand what they are, how they work, and how to deal with them. A godly response to pressure will eliminate stress during times of trial.

Pressure is externally generated; it is the force applied to you by the circumstances of life! Pressure is not an emotion, but it can give birth to emotional responses. It is felt by all of us because we all have it in varying degrees. Even little children have it. Pressure can be as simple as being hungry to the complexities of teenagers, jobs, or health issues. Pressure is motive to change! Motive to change is good, but if the change is in the wrong direction it can produce more bad results and bring on more pressure. Change to the good doesn't mean "no more pressure." It simply means a change in kind or degree. Your response to pressure is your witness of Christ to the world!

Stress is an emotional response to pressure. Pressure should never cause stress but should serve as an inventory for our view of God. Stress is generated *internally* by wrong thinking about the character of God and His purpose for us. A person who is stressed-out is exhibiting immature spiritual fruit! The character of Christ is in the fruit of the Spirit. Your level of stress when under pressure is an indicator of the maturity of the fruit of the Spirit in you. Stress is worry, and worry is the opposite of faith. A person who has realized all of God's dealings with us are ultimately for our good will not experience stress under any conditions! The mature believer will faithfully walk through high pressure situations with thanksgiving in his heart. The world generally deals with stress through drugs or psychological mumbo-jumbo. Christ deals with it by revealing Himself to us. As He reveals His faithfulness and as

He teaches that pressure is good for us, He eliminates all possibility of stress.

Trials and Reproofs

Trials are circumstances, or pressures allowed by God, to test attitudes and faith. Trials are necessary to bring about maturity. They do not come from moral collapse or personal sin, but from circumstances beyond our control... Trials come in many forms, but they are never our fault. A few examples of pain and suffering coming to a person during trials are: a person laid off from his job because his company downsizes, a crime victim, a war in our country, civil unrest, natural disaster, or temptation to sin. Trials come for causes completely outside our realm of control. That is what makes them different from reproofs.

Notice trials produce patience, and patience is a segment of the fruit of the Spirit. The fruit of the Spirit is ripened by trials. *My brethren, count it all joy when ye fall into divers temptations; Knowing this, that the trying of your faith worketh patience. But let patience have her perfect work, that ye may be perfect and entire, wanting nothing.* (James 1:2-4)

A *reproof* is what happens when life proves your ideas or your actions wrong. Rebuke and reproof are often used interchangeably, but they really are different. A rebuke is a verbal reprimand, where reproof is something happening in life when your ideas or actions do not conform to ultimate truth. For example, some reproofs for the sin of sexual immorality for example, would be: sexually transmitted disease, abortions, children out of wedlock, divorces, etc.

Trials and reproofs are different; and unless we know the difference, we will draw wrong conclusions and create confusion for ourselves. In summary:

Reproofs happen to us because we are wrong headed, or sinful.

Trials happen to us for reasons outside ourselves.

Reproofs happen as a discipline to motivate us to turn to the truth.

Trials happen in order to produce maturity and exhibit the character of Christ to the world.

Trials are circumstances that test attitudes and faith.

Reproofs should cause a turning in actions or ideas.

Trials should bring about maturity.

The following diagram will show the difference between trials and reproofs from God's perspective. The top of the diagram shows us that it is the goodness of God that leads to repentance and salvation. From the point of salvation and on through life, we have choices to make. We make countless decisions each day, and those decisions should lead us into conformity with God's purpose through obedience. But if we choose to disobey, we have a different path. We can choose to obey God or to be self-willed and go our own way.

If you will look at the diagram included here, you will be able to follow the ideas being presented. Just follow the arrows down the different paths and it won't take long to see how decision making in the Christian life has a lot of challenges. God never promised us a bed of roses either.

Decision Making for the Christian

Choices

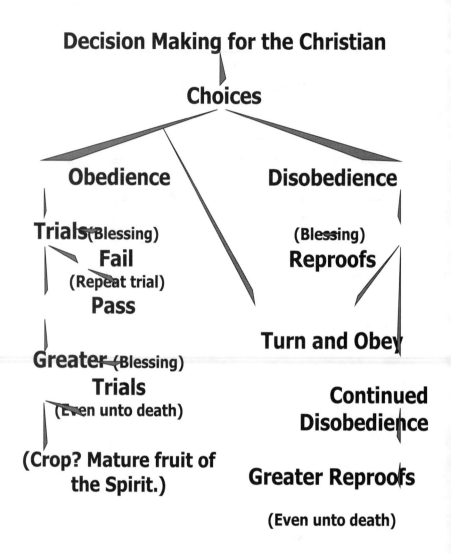

Obedience

Trials (Blessing)

Fail
(Repeat trial)
Pass

Greater (Blessing)
Trials
(Even unto death)

(Crop? Mature fruit of
the Spirit.)

Disobedience

(Blessing)
Reproofs

Turn and Obey

**Continued
Disobedience**

Greater Reproofs

(Even unto death)

The path of disobedience leads us to *reproofs of life.* Reproofs are always painful experiences, but the pain is a blessing from the Lord designed to make us turn and obey. If, at that point we do not turn and obey, we will suffer greater reproofs and greater pain and suffering. Each painful event is a blessed warning from God to repent and obey. Reproof can be even unto physical death. Pain and suffering are blessings as reproofs because they are there to lead us onto the right path. Even a reproof unto death is a blessing as a last resort, because death will stop the bad behavior.

The path of obedience also leads to pain and suffering, but in the form of trials. The trials are designed to mature the fruit of the Spirit within us and to lead us to Christlikeness. The trials will be small at first and will never be more than we can bare. As we learn to trust Him during trials, the fruit of the Spirit will mature. If we do not trust Him, we will continue to suffer the same type of trial until we do learn. Once we have learned and the fruit has matured, He will take us on to greater and more complex trials to facilitate more maturity. So, you can see trials are also blessings from God.

Are you beginning to see that no matter whether the situation is a trial or a reproof it is good and worth going through? It is God's *agapé* in action! It goes right back to Romans 8:28. *God works all things together for our good.* From God's perspective, nothing bad can happen to a Christian! God will always give you what you need in spite of what you want.

Problems come when people confuse a trial with a reproof! There are many times when we go through a trial and think it is a reproof. This is the genesis of the trite old religious statement, "You must have sin in your life." With this mistake, you can miss the opportunity to grow to maturity while you are trying to figure out which of the multitude of sins in your life has caused you to fall into this problem. Beaten down, guilt-ridden souls who are functionally out of the battle go around saying, "What have I done to deserve this?"

On the other hand, if you are going through something because you are wrongheaded or have done something wrong and you think it is a trial, you miss the opportunity to find the truth and to correct your mistakes. This is often the case when wrong headed

Christians go around complaining about the *crosses* they bear. These situations are not crosses at all, but *crops* being harvested! These are the ones who are Christian wrecking balls with disaster following them around. They are deceived by a religious spirit into seeing themselves as righteous because of all the persecution they endure. Stupidity, pride, and ignorance beget reproof; while knowledge, understanding, and wisdom beget trials.

Both trials and reproof are *agapé* in action, because they motivate change. Both of them are good for us and are blessings from God. Trials and reproofs are indeed painful pressures, but when we see they are blessings from God, it is very unlikely they will produce stress in our lives.

So why are Christians so stressed out? They don't know the purpose for trials and reproofs, and they don't know the difference between them. Both are designed to produce obedience, and only the uninformed Christian will let those pressures cause him to lose his joy in the Lord.

How can we know the difference? Such knowledge comes from Spiritual communication. Spiritual discernment is the key.

Conscience, Communion and Intuition

But the anointing which ye have received of him abideth in you, and ye need not that any man teach you: but as the same anointing teacheth you of all things, and is truth, and is no lie, and even as it hath taught you, ye shall abide in him (I John 2:27).

Spiritual discernment means: to detect or to gain knowledge by spiritual means. Spiritual discernment requires spiritual communication; and spiritual communication comes in the form of conscience, communion, and intuition. Christians have the mind of Christ; and as I John 2:27 says, we have the anointing and do not need anyone to teach us. When it come to spiritual matters, we do not learn, we simply *know*. Normal human learning takes place within a brain, but spiritual learning takes place in the spirit. Spiritual knowledge is not learned, it is revealed from spirit to spirit. The spiritual vehicles or tools with which we communicate are conscience, intuition, and communion.

The *conscience* tells us right from wrong. We do not have to learn right from wrong; we simply *know* it through our conscience. We have all felt pangs of conscience. And most of us have been in situations were there was no clearly defined right answer in the physical, but we just *knew* what was right in that instance. That knowledge came through the conscience.

The *intuition* is the organ through which we hear revelation telling us what to do in all the different situations of life. A well functioning *intuition* will mean the difference between life and death for many of us in the not too distant future. We may need to *know* who our real friends are or whether to show up at a certain place or not. We need to *know* when to speak and what to say at critical times, and the *intuition* is the organ through which that knowledge must pass.

The tool of *communion* is the most vital of all. This is the one that connects us to the mind, and power of God. *Communion* is the vehicle through which we *know* God Himself. It is through communion we learn His faithfulness, mercy, and compassion. *Communion* is the tool we use to converse, share our feelings, and explore His mind. It is through communion we receive the joy of the Lord.

We know what is right and wrong in our *conscience*; we know what to do in life's situations *intuitively;* and we facilitate conscience and intuition through *communion* with Him.

But no spiritual tool or vehicle will work unless we are quiet and peaceful enough to use it. Unless we are quietly resting and listening, reading His Word, waiting on Him and renewing our strength, our spiritual organs will fail. When our spiritual organs fail, discernment will stop. If we cannot properly discern His Spirit, we can misread pain and suffering. If we misread pain and suffering, we will lose our ability to make trustworthy decisions because our motives might be wrong. An unreliable decision making capacity is not a good witness for Christ and is a danger to those around us.

Painful things are going to happen to Christians, but none of these are seen as bad from God's perspective! It is those who have no pain and suffering who are really in trouble. He chastens the ones He loves through reproofs and trials!

It is the goodness of God that lead us to repentance (Romans 2:4)! All things start with the goodness of God! He is good; and, in Romans 11:29 we are told His gifts and calling are irrevocable. This includes salvation. It all begins with Him and ends with Him, the *Author and Finisher of our faith* (Hebrews 12:2).

Motives determine choices, and a clear understanding of God's motives gives us the ability to check ours against His. When we understand His motive (*agapé*) and conform our purpose to His, there is no fear. *Perfect love casts out all fear* (1 John 4:18).

We are living in a time when fear, or threat of loss, is commonplace, even among Christians. So how are Christians supposed to deal with the threat of loss?

Whose Is It Anyway?

You and I, everything, and everyone in the universe belong to God. This is of paramount importance and a fact that should never leave our consciousness. The moment we start to think in terms of *mine*, we begin the err. Granted, you and I have been given stewardship over certain people and things, but they do not belong to us. Life, property, and even time are God's alone; and once we begin to see it His way, all other things begin to come into focus. Anger and anxiety will leave, and peace will begin to rule. When peace reigns in our lives, thoughts become clear and right and emotions cease to be our drivers. When emotions drive actions, the actions have a tendency to be wrong. Emotions have no mind. If you do not believe that, just watch yourself the next time you see a frightening or exciting movie. You will find your body reacting emotionally to light on a piece of canvas while you know what you are seeing is not real! Your emotions don't know the difference between reality and fiction. Anger, fear (with the exception of the natural fight or flight reaction), joy, or any other emotion should never be a motive for action. *Agapé* is the only proper motive for action, and *agapé* is not an emotion! One should always question actions motivated by emotion.

76

The Lord has provided a way for us to quench emotional decision making. The method is simple and I will give you an example. Let's say a man steals *my* car. If it is *my* car, then I will get really angry at first and want to retaliate. Then I will go into an episode of grieving over the loss, once I recognize the reality of the situation. You see, anger comes only by one thing, *threat of loss*. Losing something does not cause anger, losing something causes us to grieve. It is only the threat of loss that causes anger. If I have nothing to lose, then anger has no power over me. If the Lord wants a man to steal *His* car and the Lord wants me to use the money which He provides me to buy another one, then that is the Lord's business. No anger and minimal grief occur here. Do you ever get angry at the guy who sits through a green light? Maybe you have the idea that time belongs to you. *My* time, *my* property, *my* life....no, not really! Everything will operate better once we realize all things are His because people have a tendency to take better care of the Lords' property than their own.

If you haven't done so before, now is the time to acknowledge the Lord's ownership of everything. Now is the time to tell Him you understand all things are His. Ask Him to make you a proper steward of the time, people, and possessions He has placed under your stewardship. Only when you have done that are you ready for the next step.

So then, how does one go about making decisions once he realizes that all things belong to God and man's only responsibility is proper stewardship? What exactly is God's purpose for us in all this? What are we supposed to do and be like before the world? Since He is the manufacturer, He is the only one qualified to give us answers to these questions. The Lord has set down certain general functions of stewardship for us in His Word. We all have our conscience and intuition, but it is communion that first facilitates His knowledge. Communion begins with His written *Word* and ends with prayer and meditation. He has given us certain general functions of stewardship in His Word: Here are a few examples:

Never do what *you* think is right: This may be the most

difficult of all!

> Deuteronomy 12:8 – *Ye shall not do after all the things that we do here this day, every man whatsoever is right in his own eyes.* The Book is full of examples of the wrongheadedness of men when they do what they think is right. When men do what is right in their own eyes chaos is always the result.

> Judges 17:6 – *In those days there was no king in Israel, but every man did that which was right in his own eyes.*

> Proverbs 16:25 – *There is a way that seemeth right unto a man, but the end thereof are the ways of death.*

Do what is good and right in the eyes of the Lord.

> Deuteronomy 12:28 – *Observe and hear all these words which I command thee, that it may go well with thee, and with thy children after thee for ever, when thou doest that which is good and right in the sight of the LORD thy God.*

Don't fight with unbelievers.

> Proverbs 29:9 – *If a wise man contendeth with a foolish man, whether he rage or laugh, there is no rest.* Francis of Assisi said it well when he said, "Preach the gospel all the time and when necessary use words."

Remember, you have been sent here for this time as an ambassador for Christ!

> Proverbs 22:20-21 – *Have not I written to thee excellent things in counsels and knowledge, That I might make thee know the certainty of the words of truth; that thou mightest answer the words of truth to them that send unto thee?*

> 2 Corinthians 5:18-21 – *And all things are of God, who hath reconciled us to himself by Jesus Christ, and hath given to us the ministry of reconciliation; To wit, that God was in Christ, reconciling the world unto himself, not imputing their trespasses unto them; and hath committed unto us the word of*

reconciliation. Now then we are ambassadors for Christ, as though God did beseech you by us: we pray you in Christ's stead, be ye reconciled to God. For he hath made him to be sin for us, who knew no sin; that we might be made the righteousness of God in him.

Consider the cause of the poor.

Proverbs 28:27 – *He that giveth unto the poor shall not lack: but he that hideth his eyes shall have many a curse.*

Proverbs 11:26 – *He that withholdeth corn, the people shall curse him: but blessing shall be upon the head of him that selleth it.*

Isaiah 58:6-7 – *Is not this the fast that I have chosen? to loose the bands of wickedness, to undo the heavy burdens, and to let the oppressed go free, and that ye break every yoke? Is it not to deal thy bread to the hungry, and that thou bring the poor that are cast out to thy house? when thou seest the naked, that thou cover him; and that thou hide not thyself from thine own flesh?*

Trust the Lord and don't be afraid.

Proverbs 18:10 – *The name of the LORD is a strong tower: the righteous runneth into it, and is safe.*

Proverbs 3:5-6 – *Trust in the LORD with all thine heart; and lean not unto thine own understanding. In all thy ways acknowledge him, and he shall direct thy paths.*

Prepare as the Lord leads.

Proverbs 22:3 – *A prudent man foreseeth the evil, and hideth himself: but the simple pass on, and are punished.* (Note: this Proverb repeats in Proverbs 27:12, giving double impact to the instruction.)

I Timothy 5:8 – *But if any provide not for his own, and specially for those of his own house, he hath denied the faith, and is worse than an infidel.*

You are called to defend those who can't defend

79

themselves.

Proverbs 31:8-9 – *Open thy mouth for the dumb in the cause of all such as are appointed to destruction. Open thy mouth, judge righteously, and plead the cause of the poor and needy.*

Psalms 82:3-4 – *Defend the poor and fatherless: do justice to the afflicted and needy. Deliver the poor and needy: rid them out of the hand of the wicked.*

Isaiah 1:17 – *Learn to do well; seek judgment, relieve the oppressed, judge the fatherless, plead for the widow.* God will be defending us while we defend the defenseless!

Psalms 20:1 – *The LORD hear thee in the day of trouble; the name of the God of Jacob defend thee;* The Lord rebukes those who refuse to defend the helpless.

Jeremiah 5:26-28 – *For among my people are found wicked men: they lay wait, as he that setteth snares; they set a trap, they catch men. As a cage is full of birds, so are their houses full of deceit: therefore they are become great, and waxen rich. They are waxen fat, they shine: yea, they overpass the deeds of the wicked: they judge not the cause, the cause of the fatherless, yet they prosper; and the right of the needy do they not judge.*

Each of us has a duty to obey God, and if obedience calls for self-sacrifice then so be it. We must do as the Lord directs. We have the right to lay down our lives for Christ.

However, we do not have the right to let someone else take life and property from others when it is in the power of our hand to prevent it. If someone asks for assistance, we must give of our God given resources to obey the command to feed ,clothe, and provide dwelling place for the needy. If, on the other hand someone tries to take from others by force, then that person must be resisted, by force if necessary! Hopefully the use of force to protect the innocent will not become necessary; but if it does, we must be prepared to use it as the Lord directs. Only by constant communion with the Lord will we know for sure when force is necessary. These decisions will be made on the spur of the moment. One must have a close, meaningful, and listening relationship with the Lord to do the right thing in violent times. Pray the Lord will guide you in these instances.

Remember...All believers are overcomers.

> Isaiah 54:16-17 – *Behold, I have created the smith that bloweth the coals in the fire, and that bringeth forth an instrument for his work; and I have created the waster to destroy. No weapon that is formed against thee shall prosper; and every tongue that shall rise against thee in judgment thou shalt condemn. This is the heritage of the servants of the LORD, and their righteousness is of me, saith the LORD.*

> Isaiah 40:28-29 – *Hast thou not known? hast thou not heard, that the everlasting God, the LORD, the Creator of the ends of the earth, fainteth not, neither is weary? there is no searching of his understanding. He giveth power to the faint; and to them that have no might he increaseth strength.*

> I John 5:4-5 – *For whatsoever is born of God overcometh the world: and this is the victory that overcometh the world, even our faith. Who is he that overcometh the world, but he that believeth that Jesus is the Son of God?*

Know that you are forever safe in Him.

> Psalms 27:1-5 – *The LORD is my light and my salvation; whom shall I fear? the LORD is the strength of my life; of whom shall I be afraid? When the wicked, even mine enemies and my foes, came upon me to eat up my flesh, they stumbled and fell. Though an host should encamp against me, my heart shall not fear: though war should rise against me, in this will I be confident. One thing have I desired of the LORD, that will I seek after; that I may dwell in the house of the LORD all the*

days of my life, to behold the beauty of the LORD, and to inquire in his temple. For in the time of trouble he shall hide me in his pavilion: in the secret of his tabernacle shall he hide me; he shall set me up upon a rock.

Know His voice and stay in His word.

This is the key to making discerning choices on an instantaneous basis.

Psalms 119:105 – *Thy word is a lamp unto my feet, and a light unto my path.*

John 10:27 – *My sheep hear my voice, and I know them, and they follow me:*

Right moral choices will be automatic for you, if you are at peace and trusting in Him, knowing His word, and hearing His voice. When times are confusing, pressure is constant, and uncertainty is the order of the day, our Lord has a personal word for you. *Rejoice in the Lord alway: and again I say, Rejoice. Let your moderation be known unto all men. The Lord is at hand. Be careful for nothing; but in every thing by prayer and supplication with thanksgiving let your requests be made known unto God. And the peace of God, which passeth all understanding, shall keep your hearts and minds through Christ Jesus. Finally, brethren, whatsoever things are true, whatsoever things are honest, whatsoever things are just, whatsoever things are pure, whatsoever things are lovely, whatsoever things are of good report; if there be any virtue, and if there be any praise, think on these things. Not that I speak in respect of want: for I have learned, in whatsoever state I am, therewith to be content. I know both how to be abased, and I know how to abound: every where and in all things I am instructed both to be full and to be hungry, both to abound and to suffer need. I can do all things through Christ which strengtheneth me. But my God shall supply all your need according to his riches in glory by Christ Jesus. Now unto God and our Father be glory for ever and ever. Amen. (Philippians* 4:4-8, 11-13, 19-20)

As you can see, God really expects us to shine in trials – to shine so the world can see Him through us. He also wants us to remember we are just visitors here and we are His ambassadors. I believe C.S. Lewis put it beautifully when he said, "We ought to give thanks for all fortune: if it is 'good,' because it is good, if it is 'bad,' because it works in us patience, humility and the contempt of this world and the hope of our eternal country."

Chapter 5

"If I Perish, I Perish"
Michael Bunker

Overcoming

What characteristics of the martyrs of the past allowed them to stand firm in the face of persecution? What personal attributes can be ascribed to those who successfully proclaimed Christ - even to their own peril?

It is vital that we note here, that *it is impossible for us to fail!* We must realize that Christ will be glorified, and His will WILL be done, regardless of our actions on His behalf. To think that our behavior in the face of persecution lessens or increases Christ's glory is just prideful silliness on our part which must be avoided. Our patience and steadfastness in the face of persecution and villainy is a product of Christ's work *in* us - not our work *for* Christ. We are not a participant in the work, we are a PRODUCT of it! Our ability to withstand is a testimony of the greatness of our LORD and His faith which he has placed in us, not in our greatness in engaging in "self-control". Demons can allow a man to withstand torture and undergo pain and death, however, this is not what Christ defines as overcoming. Overcoming is an *end product* and it is finally defined by how our lives and ideas line up with the will of the Creator. Our admission as believers that we are unable to accomplish *anything* outside of the direction and control of Christ is the primary means by which we are able to submit ourselves to

His greater plan.

Admitting that Jesus is in charge, accepting that whatever becomes of us is GOOD for us and is according to His plan, submitting to His authority while understanding that Christ is serving our best interests in times of trouble - these are the things that allow us to be seen by the world as "more than overcomers". This is why we say that it is IMPOSSIBLE for us to fail. If we are weak and we succumb to pressure - it glorifies Christ that He has chosen to redeem and show grace and mercy to such broken vessels. If we are strong and show courage, it is a manifestation of the greatness of Christ that He is able to lift us up above the evils of our nature, so that all of the angels and principalities and powers are awed by what He has accomplished with *mere dirt from the ground.*

Christ, from the beginning, has been glorified in His creation. He is, at His core, a CREATOR - and when mere man is able to reflect the glory of the Creator - GOD Himself is glorified in the doing of it. Peter was not lost by his denial of Christ, neither was he saved by his martyrdom in Rome. Peter was saved when he properly answered Jesus' question, "Whom say ye that I am?" From Christ's death through Peter's murder in Rome, Peter, as a "born again" child of the living GOD, was righteous in the sight of his Creator. By overcoming; by being obedient to his own martyrdom; by resisting evil - Peter was a witness to those who would follow. We CANNOT fail!

****

It is only through the denial of self and submission to Christ's Holy work in us that we become sensitive to His voice. As we have shown in the previous chapters, like Christ, we learn obedience through the things that we suffer. *Suffering* teaches *obedience*, *obedience* opens the ears so that we may *hear*, *hearing* opens the door to *wisdom* and *understanding.* The martyrs of the past centuries were wise enough to understand that persecution was GOOD for them! They understood that temporal pain and discomfort would be forgotten during eternity in Christ's presence.

Obedience allowed them to separate themselves from their physical flesh long enough to see themselves, GOD, and others through GOD's eyes! This is the definition we have given of *humility*. Humility is welcome in the presence of the Lord. Pride is not! Pride gives us a broken human view of our situation. Humility gives us a perfected Godly view of our situation. Richard Wurmbrand, who wrote *Tortured For Christ*, was able to see his incarceration and torture through GOD's eyes. This allowed him to overcome in his situation. He perservered. Had Wurmbrand chosen to view his situation through his own eyes, he would have quickly lost all hope, and he would have succumbed.

****

What does Overcoming look like?

One of the greatest men I ever met was the late evangelist David Busby. David was born with Cystic Fibrosis and also suffered from Polio as a child. Most Cystic Fibrosis patients are fortunate to live into their 20's, but when I heard David preach, he was in his mid-40's. He weighed about 80 lbs. soaking wet, and he resembled a man on his deathbed.

When David came to speak at my home church in Lubbock, Texas, he had to be rolled into the church in a wheel chair. During his four day stay in Lubbock, he was rushed to the hospital emergency room three separate times. He had 15% of his lung capacity left. Each evening after preaching, he coughed up blood. Each night, he was strapped to a breathing machine for three hours.

With all of these obvious hardships and handicaps, I noticed some shocking things about David Busby that I shall never forget. He was funny, he was joyful, and he had absolutely NO FEAR!

****

David Busby was not travelling around the country preaching the gospel because he wanted to *earn* his way into heaven. He was not a man on his deathbed frantically trying to convince Jesus that he was worthy of salvation. David knew he was not worthy. David was convinced of his moral bankruptcy. He knew he was going to heaven based on the mercy and grace of Jesus Christ alone, due to Christ's obedience to His death on the cross. David had accepted resurrected LIFE from Jesus. Consequently, he had nothing to fear. He stepped out into LIFE daily, completely convinced that GOD held him securely, completely aware that there was no pressure on him to perform, and that because of this - he was free to BEAR FRUIT to a dying world. David Busby bore fruit joyfully - he truly reflected the glory of Jesus Christ. Dave is in heaven because GOD is good, not because Dave was. This emaciated, dying man was more than an overcomer during a life that most of us could not even imagine. He suffered more pain and discomfort than I can even conceive. He was able to do so because he was *convinced* of the character of his Creator, and he understood that GOD was performing a great work in and through him, as He is in each and every believer.

In one of David's last talks, he said, "I have been healed of the need to be healed, and if I die the most painful and horrible death possible - strapped to a hospital bed, breathing air through a tube - I will KNOW that GOD is great, and that HE is merciful, and that my death was *perfect*." (That is exactly how he died)

I can't tell you how much that statement means to me. It impressed on me the vital necessity of *endurance*. Paul spoke often of endurance in his epistles - likening the Christian life to a road race that must be run. He did not liken the race to works, but to obedience to the voice of the Creator. It seems to me that we are blind runners in a darkened maze. Hearing the voice of the Lord is so vital to our existence that without it we become confused and frightened mice, cowering in a corner, praying for more light. The scriptures say that WE are to be salt and light to a dark and dying world. Hearing GOD's voice keeps us functional, effective and powerful in the times we face.

****

David Busby now sits with Jesus Christ and gets to see the whole world situation like GOD sees it - outside of our temporal limitations of time and space. He can see the brilliance of GOD's plan unfold, and for the first time, he can see his own role in it. It is *this view*, GOD's perspective, that brings our individual fates into closer focus. From GOD's point of view, ALL things are working together for good for those who love Him. ALL THINGS!!

The topics we have discussed in this book; persecution, tyranny, evil, resistance, obedience, joy, etc. are all a part of GOD's Holy plan for the redemption of his chosen people. We are not told to win, we are told to STRIVE. We are not told to defeat evil (that is Jesus' job), we are told to RESIST. GOD is very clear about our position in these events - We are to obey! Our ways are not His ways, and His ways are not our ways.

****

"Then Esther bade them return Mordechai this answer, Go gather together all the Jews that are present in Shushan, and fast ye for me, and neither eat nor drink three days, night or day: I also and my maidens will fast likewise; and so will I go in unto the king, which is not according to the law, and if I perish, I perish." Esther 4:15,16

Mordechai had asked Esther to go into the court of King Ahasuerus and intercede on behalf of the Jews, because unbeknownst to the King, Esther was a Jew. It seems that one of the King's men, an evil man by the name of Haman had conspired to murder all of the Jews in the land. Esther informed Mordechai that it was unlawful to go into the King when one had not been called, and that the penalty for such behavior was death. Unless, of course, the King was to extend his golden scepter in peace to the guest - in which case the life of the visitor would be spared.

Mordechai's answer to Esther is profound:

"For if thou altogether holdest thy peace at this time, then shall deliverance arise to the Jews from another place; but thou and thy fathers house shall be destroyed: and who knoweth whether thou art come to the kingdom for such a time as this?" Esther 4:14

This is amazing! Mordechai tells Esther, "Listen, if you aren't obedient to the Lord and if you don't intercede for the Jews, GOD will raise up someone ELSE who will!" Mordechai is saying to Esther, "THIS IS NOT ABOUT YOU!, GOD WILL BE GLORIFIED AND VICTORIOUS IF YOU PARTICIPATE OR NOT!"

Esther's response is classic, and should remain on the tip of our tongues as we enter into a time that screams out for the obedience of GOD's people:

She said, "I'll do it", and then:

"If I perish, I perish."

Contrast that response with that of the Christian pastors in Rwanda that we talked about in Chapter 1. Those pastors, when they found themselves in harm's way, turned their flocks over to be slaughtered in order to save their own lives. We need more MEN like Esther!!

****

Who knows whether we have come to the Kingdom for such a time as this? Many people spend their entire lives searching for *why* GOD created them. For Stephen, the first Christian martyr, his purpose is depicted for us in the Book of Acts, chapter 7. Stephen lived almost all of his life in obscurity, but the Lord called him forth in a moment of *dire* importance to the young Christian faith - Stephen was called to speak the truth to the Scribes and

Pharisees.

For speaking the truth, Stephen was immediately stoned to death - martyred for Christ. Stephen was created for such a moment, and he was obedient to the voice of the Lord in a time when most of us would have vacillated or fled.

The Bible is replete with such stories. GOD calls forth those that He chooses for critical moments in time. And as Mordechai would say, "IT'S NOT ABOUT US."

We must heed the voice of GOD. We must be obedient to that "still, small voice" of the SPIRIT of GOD. If and when the Creator calls us forth, we will then recognize His voice and respond accordingly. But always remember - WE CANNOT FAIL! GOD is victorious, we already know the end of the story! And if we perish, we perish. Who knows - GOD may have called YOU for such a time as this.

Chapter 6

Persecution 2000
Michael Bunker

"The Church underground is the Church of one third of the world, men who had never thought before that they would have to belong to an underground Church. While America was preoccupied with Watergate, Communists took over fifteen countries. Christian pastors must know what an underground Church looks like and what it does." Pastor Richard Wurmbrand, Preparing for the Underground Church. Voice of the Martyrs.

The Gathering Clouds

Most Christians today believe that something is desperately wrong in America - and in the world. It is the Holy Spirit of the Lord in us that commands us to "WATCH!". By connecting the dots - watching world events, studying prophetic scriptures, understanding the "signs of the times", believers everywhere are on full alert. Many have been lulled into complacency and apathy by a corrupt and dying church "corporation" that has as it's prime motivation "self-preservation".

Martin Niemoller approached Adolph Hitler in 1936 and wagged a bony prophetic finger in his face and proclaimed, "Sir, it is not the church we are worried about. Jesus Christ will well take care of His church. What we are concerned about, Sir, is the very *soul* of our nation." - Niemoller was quite alone in his proclamation. The rest of the pastors and church leaders hushed him and spirited him from the room. They were too concerned about the tax breaks and subsidies that Hitler had promised to them. Years later as the bodies piled up in Germany (Niemoller's own was atop the pile at Auschwitz), the corrupt pastors would wipe the dust from the Nazi ovens off of their cars as they left for church on Sunday morning.

After hearing this story, I proclaimed to a Bible study group that, "The Christian church should have been fighting and dying, not in 1943 as the Jews were hauled to the ovens in Germany, but in 1933 when Hitler called for the banning of all private gun ownership in the country." I stand by that proclamation. The Christian Church in Germany was unable to obey the Biblical command to "defend the defenseless", because they traded their right to defense for a few more years of cowardice and fear. Would it have been better to have died for a righteous cause in 1933, or to have waited another 10-12 years to watch your own freedom, and the freedom of millions of others be stripped from you at the hand of despotic government?

Persecution will come to America because we deserve no better. The warning shouts of our forefathers echo from heaven as the monstrous death machine of international tyranny thunders into action. The lessons of Rwanda and Egypt and Mexico are brushed under the corporate rug, as the death tolls mount on the plains of the Sudan. At this writing our government is push button murdering thousands of Greek Orthodox Christians in Serbia/Yugoslavia. Their deaths come as "fire from the sky", as American bombers launch cruise missiles on homes and schools and factories - all from hundreds of miles away. Days ago, two lone gunman (children) opened fire with guns and bombs in a high school in Colorado, killing scores of children and teachers. The stories that most of the dead were born-again believers cannot be discounted. GOD has handed our nation over to a reprobate mind. Evil men rule over us. But we deserve no better.

"Hear this, ye old men, and give ear, all ye inhabitants of

the land. Hath this been in your days, or even in the days of your fathers? Tell ye your children of it, and let your children tell their children, and their children another generation. That which the palmerworm hath left hath the locust eaten; and that which the locust hath left hat the cankerworm eaten; and that which the cankerworm hath left hath the caterpiller eaten. Awake, ye drunkards, and weep; and howl, all ye drinkers of wine, because of the new wine; for it is cut off from your mouth. For a nation is come up upon my land, strong, and without number, whose teeth are the teeth of a lion, and he hath the cheek teeth of a great lion. He hath laid my vine waste, and barked my fig tree: he hath made it clean bare, and cast it away; the branches thereof are made white. Lament like a virgin girded with sackcloth for the husband of her youth." (Joel 1:2-8)

When persecution comes in full form to America, how are Christians to respond? One thing we have tried to make perfectly clear is that each and every believer is a fully functioning part of the body. We are not about to tell anyone what they should or should not do in response to tyranny. Listening to GOD and obeying His voice is our primary goal. But are there any "rules of thumb"? Are there any general guidelines that we can follow?

Richard Wurmbrand suggests in his pamphlet, *Preparing for the Underground Church*, that preparation "begins with studying *sufferology*, martyrology, Solzhenitsyn, in his book *Gulag Archipelago* says that police officers in the former Soviet Union had a course on *arrestology* - the science of how to arrest people so that nobody around shall observe. If they have created a new name, arrestology, let us create the name of *sufferology*."

I think that he is right. Studying the works and writings of those who have already been subject to persecution is a good way to learn how persecution might manifest itself. I think if more people were students of history, we wouldn't be in this jam to begin with. Unfortunately, there aren't many books on *sufferology*, or on Underground Churches at all. The greatest book we can study on the subject is the Bible.

Here are some ideas:

1. Be very circumspect and pray diligently about who you choose to befriend during troubled times. Being a servant of Christ and serving the best interests of others is one thing, unloading all of your personal information on strangers is another. During times of trouble, it is best to adopt a *need to know policy*. Governments do it all of the time.

2. Study diligently about underground movements. Start with the underground railroad here in the US during the civil war. How did small groups of people and individuals perform their acts of heroism when death was the penalty? Read about the underground movements in Italy during World War II, and in France during that same war.

3. Decide BEFOREHAND what you will or will not put up with as a Christian. It is too late when thugs begin to harass your neighbors, to develop a consistent and GODLY opinion on harassment. Decide BEFOREHAND what you will or will not say to "authorities" if you are illegally questioned or incarcerated. Decide BEFOREHAND what your response will be to any number of unacceptable behaviors by the government. Decide BEFOREHAND to accept whatever tortures or indecencies are inflicted upon you by your adversaries - WITHOUT giving out information on your friends and allies. Wurmbrand says it thus, "But what about the terrible tortures which are inflicted on prisoners? What will we do about these tortures? Will we be able to bear them? If I do NOT bear them, I put in prison another fifty or sixty men whom I know because that is what the oppressors wish from me, to betray those around me."

4. Speak openly of your faith in Jesus Christ, but not so openly of WHERE and WHEN your brethren meet to worship him, or to plan resistance to those who would persecute you. We do not speak here of the "corporation" that we call churches. We speak of the brotherhood of Christian believers called "the Body".

5. Watch and pray diligently, that you might be aware when wolves try to enter into the sheepfold. There are traitors everywhere. Jesus had one in his group, it is likely you do too.

6. Study "Leaderless Resistance". Although we as believers are never leaderless, the time has come when having human leaders is too dangerous. The enemy rejoices at "lopping off the head", so we must learn to function like the cells in the body, with Christ only as the "leader".

7. Stand firm for those things which Christ has taught you in your spirit. The days of compromise in the Christian faith are over. Realize that victorious faith is a gift from GOD, so use it! Come to the realization that you are only a cell in the Body of Christ. The Body is large, and it is diverse - we do not compromise on the TRUTH of the gospel, be we must FEEL it when a diverse part of the body is being persecuted.

8. Most of all - BE OBEDIENT! You will hear the voice of GOD like never before in your life. Christ is calling for instantaneous obedience. This is how the Bride will shine in days of darkness. We are salt and light. It is time for the bride to shine!

****

Most of all it is our hope, and most fervent prayer that you overcome in times of adversity. This book was designed to help you understand some of the events that led us to where we are today as a nation, and as a Body. If it were possible that we might pass through these trying times unscathed, I don't know that I would wish for it. If maintaining the "status quo" means that we as a nation maintain our downward slide from the lofty heights our forefathers built for us, then I for one am praying for "rock bottom". If deep inside your spirit, there is not a stirring - a feeling that the time has come for the Bride to awaken and watch diligently for her Husband, then read again Chapters 2-4 about how the Bride is to truly function. Our hearts quicken at the thought of our Lord's soon return. But until then, we are admonished to WATCH! Hard times are coming, in fact, they are already upon us. The time is short. There is no longer time to vacillate between two gods. Choose ye this day which God you will serve!

As for me and my house - We will serve the Lord!

"Even so, come, Lord Jesus."